Federal Benefits for Veterans and Dependents

2005 Edition

Department of Veterans Affairs

Office of Public Affairs (80D)
810 Vermont Ave., N.W.
Washington, DC 20420

For sale by the Superintendent of Documents, U.S. Government Printing Office
Internet: bookstore.gpo.gov Phone: toll free (866) 512-1800; DC area (202) 512-1800
Fax: (202) 512-2250 Mail: Stop SSOP, Washington, DC 20402-0001

ISBN 0-16-051588-2

Contents

Introduction 1
   Wartime Service 2
   Special Groups 2
   Selected Reserve and National Guard 4
   Filipino Veterans 4
   Important Documents 5
   Privacy Act 5
   Introduction in Spanish 5

Health Care Benefits 6
   Health Care Enrollment 6
      Priority Groups 6
      Special Access to Care 8
   Financial Information 8
      Financial Assessment 8
      Services Requiring Copayments 9
      Outpatient Visits Not Requiring Copayments 9
      Billing Insurance Companies 10
   Health Care Programs 10
   Veteran Health Registries 10
      Gulf War Registry 10
      Depleted Uranium Registries 10
      Agent Orange Registry 10
      Ionizing Radiation Registry 11
   Readjustment Counseling Service 11
   Prosthetic and Sensory Aid Services 12
   Services and Aids for Blind Veterans 12
   Home Improvements and Structural Alterations 12
   Alcohol and Drug-Dependence Treatment 13
   Compensated Work Therapy 13
   Outpatient Dental Treatment 13
   Outpatient Pharmacy Services 14
   Nursing-Home Care 15
   Domiciliary Care 16
   Medical Care for Dependents and Survivors 16
   Beneficiary Travel 17
   Emergency Medical Care in Non-VA Facilities 17
   Veterans Living or Traveling Overseas 18
   Merchant Marine Seamen 18
   Allied Veterans 18

Benefit Programs 19
  Disability Compensation 19
    Receiving Benefit Payments 19
    Prisoners of War 19
    Agent Orange and Other Herbicides 20
    Veterans Exposed to Radiation 20
    Gulf War Veterans 20
    Specially Adapted Homes 21
    Automobile Assistance 22
    Clothing Allowance 22
    Allowances for Dependents 23
    Aid and Attendance or Housebound 23
    Incarcerated Veterans 23
    Fugitive Felons 23
  Pension 23
    Improved Pension 24
    Protected Pension Programs 24
    Medal of Honor Pension 24
  Vocational Rehabilitation and Employment 24
    Services 25
  Children of Vietnam Veterans Born with Certain Birth Defects 26
    Spina Bifida Program 26
    Children of Women Vietnam Veterans Program 27
  Education and Training 28
    Montgomery GI Bill 28
    Montgomery GI Bill - Selected Reserve 33
    Veterans' Educational Assistance Program (VEAP) 34
  Home Loan Guaranties 36
    Eligibility 36
    Guaranty Amount 39
    Required Occupancy 39
    Closing Costs 40
    Financing, Interest Rates and Terms 40
    Release of Liability, Loan Assumption 41
    Loans for Native American Veterans 41
    Repossessed Homes 42
    Safeguards for Veterans 42
  Life Insurance 43
    Servicemembers' Group Life Insurance 43
    Family Servicemembers' Group Life Insurance 43
    Veterans' Group Life Insurance 44
    Accelerated Death Benefits for SGLI, FSGLI and VGLI 44
    Service-Disabled Veterans Insurance 44

Veterans' Mortgage Life Insurance 45
Insurance Dividends 45
Miscellaneous Insurance Information 45

Burial Benefits 47
Eligibility 47
Burial in VA National Cemeteries 47
Headstones and Markers 48
Presidential Memorial Certificates 49
Burial Flags 49
Reimbursement of Burial Expenses 50
Military Funeral Honors 50
Veterans Cemeteries Administered by Other Agencies 51
  Arlington National Cemetery 51
  Department of the Interior 51
  State Veterans Cemeteries 51

Survivor Benefits 52
Dependency and Indemnity Compensation (DIC) 52
  DIC Payments to Surviving Spouse 52
  DIC Payments to Parents and Children 53
  Special Allowances 53
  Restored Entitlement Program for Survivors 53
Death Pension 53
Home Loan Guaranties 54
Dependents' Education 54
  Monthly Payments 55
  Special Benefits 55
  Montgomery GI Bill Death Benefit 56

Women Veterans 56

Homeless Veterans 57

Overseas Benefits 58
Medical Benefits 58

Small and Disadvantaged Businesses 58

Appeals 59
Board of Veterans' Appeals 59
U.S. Court of Appeals for Veterans Claims 60

Workplace Benefits 61
- Unemployment Compensation 61
- Transition Assistance Program 61
  - Pre-separation Counseling 61
  - Verification of Military Experience and Training 62
  - Transition Bulletin Board 62
  - DoD Transportal 62
- Veterans' Workforce Investment Program 62
- State Employment Services 63
- Re-employment Rights 63
- Federal Jobs for Veterans 64
  - Veterans Readjustment Appointment 65
  - Veterans' Invitational Program 65

Miscellaneous Benefits 65
- Loans for Farms and Homes 65
- Housing and Urban Development 65
- Naturalization Preference 66
- Small Business Administration 67
- Federal Tax Credits and Assistance 67
- Social Security 67
- Supplemental Security Income 68
- Passports to Visit Overseas Cemeteries 68
- Medals 69
- Review of Discharges 69
- Replacing Military Records 70
- Correction of Military Records 71
- Armed Forces Retirement Home 71
- Commissary and Exchange Privileges 72
- Death Gratuity 72

Tables 73-77

Important Phone Numbers 78

VA on the Internet 79

VA Facilities 80

Index 118

Introduction

This pamphlet describes federal benefits available to veterans and their dependents as of Jan. 1, 2005. Changes may occur during the year as a result of legislative or other requirements. The Department of Veterans Affairs (VA) World Wide Web pages (http://www.va.gov) are updated throughout the year to present the most current information. The VA Home page contains links to sections on compensation and pension, health care, burial benefits, home loan guarantees and other information.

Eligibility depends upon individual circumstances. To determine eligibility for VA health care, contact the Enrollment Coordinator at the nearest VA health care facility or call the Health Benefits Service Center at 1-877-222-8387. For other VA benefits eligibility, contact a VA benefits office at 1-800-827-1000 from any location in the United States. Assistance is also available through Telecommunication Device for the Deaf (TDD) at 1-800-829-4833. Phone numbers of VA offices, including those in the Philippines and Puerto Rico, are listed in the back of this book. VA facilities also are listed in the federal government section of telephone directories.

Eligibility for most VA benefits is based upon discharge from active military service under other than dishonorable conditions. Active service means full-time service, other than active duty for training, as a member of the Army, Navy, Air Force, Marine Corps, Coast Guard, or as a commissioned officer of the Public Health Service, the Environmental Science Services Administration or the National Oceanic and Atmospheric Administration, or its predecessor organization, the Coast and Geodectic Survey. Men and women veterans with similar service are entitled to the same VA benefits.

Honorable and general discharges qualify a veteran for most VA benefits. Dishonorable and bad conduct discharges issued by general courts-martial may bar VA benefits. Veterans in prison and parolees may be eligible for certain VA benefits. VA regional offices can clarify the eligibility of prisoners, parolees and individuals with multiple discharges issued under differing conditions. VA benefits will not be provided to any veteran or dependent wanted for an outstanding felony warrant.

Wartime Service
Certain VA benefits require wartime service. Under the law, VA recognizes these war periods:

Mexican Border Period: May 9, 1916, through April 5, 1917, for veterans who served in Mexico, on its borders or in adjacent waters.

World War I: April 6, 1917, through Nov. 11, 1918; for veterans who served in Russia, April 6, 1917, through April 1, 1920; extended through July 1, 1921, for veterans who had at least one day of service between April 6, 1917, and Nov. 11, 1918.

World War II: Dec. 7, 1941, through Dec. 31, 1946.

Korean War: June 27, 1950, through Jan. 31, 1955.

Vietnam War: Aug. 5, 1964 (Feb. 28, 1961, for veterans who served "in country" before Aug. 5, 1964), through May 7, 1975.

Gulf War: Aug. 2, 1990, through a date to be set by law or Presidential Proclamation.

Special Groups: A number of groups who have provided military-related service to the United States have been granted VA benefits. For the service to qualify, the Secretary of Defense must certify that the group has provided active military service. Individuals must be issued a discharge by the Secretary of Defense to qualify for VA benefits. Service in the following groups has been certified as active military service for benefits purposes:

1. Women Air Force Service Pilots (WASPs).
2. World War I Signal Corps Female Telephone Operators Unit.
3. Engineer Field Clerks.
4. Women's Army Auxiliary Corps (WAAC).
5. Quartermaster Corps female clerical employees serving with the American Expeditionary Forces in World War I.
6. Civilian employees of Pacific naval air bases who actively participated in defense of Wake Island during World War II.
7. Reconstruction aides and dietitians in World War I.
8. Male civilian ferry pilots.
9. Wake Island defenders from Guam.
10. Civilian personnel assigned to OSS secret intelligence.
11. Guam Combat Patrol.

12. Quartermaster Corps members of the Keswick crew on Corregidor during World War II.

13. U.S. civilians who participated in the defense of Bataan.

14. U.S. merchant seamen who served on block ships in support of Operation Mulberry in the World War II invasion of Normandy.

15. American merchant marines in oceangoing service during World War II.

16. Civilian Navy IFF radar technicians who served in combat areas of the Pacific during World War II.

17. U.S. civilians of the American Field Service who served overseas in World War I.

18. U.S. civilians of the American Field Service who served overseas under U.S. armies and U.S. army groups in World War II.

19. U.S. civilian employees of American Airlines who served overseas in a contract with the Air Transport Command between Dec. 14, 1941, and Aug. 14, 1945.

20. Civilian crewmen of U.S. Coast and Geodetic Survey vessels who served in areas of immediate military hazard while conducting cooperative operations with and for the U.S. armed forces between Dec. 7, 1941, and Aug. 15, 1945.

21. Members of the American Volunteer Group (Flying Tigers) who served between Dec. 7, 1941, and July 18, 1942.

22. U.S. civilian flight crew and aviation ground support employees of United Air Lines who served overseas in a contract with Air Transport Command between Dec. 14, 1941, and Aug. 14, 1945.

23. U.S. civilian flight crew and aviation ground support employees of Transcontinental and Western Air, Inc. (TWA), who served overseas in a contract with the Air Transport Command between Dec. 14, 1941, and Aug. 14, 1945.

24. U.S. civilian flight crew and aviation ground support employees of Consolidated Vultee Aircraft Corp. (Consairway Division) who served overseas in a contract with Air Transport Command between Dec. 14, 1941, and Aug. 14, 1945.

25. U.S. civilian flight crew and aviation ground support employees of Pan American World Airways and its subsidiaries and affiliates, who served overseas in a contract with the Air Transport Command and Naval Air Transport Service between Dec. 14, 1941, and Aug. 14, 1945.

26. Honorably discharged members of the American Volunteer Guard, Eritrea Service Command, between June 21, 1942, and March 31, 1943.

27. U.S. civilian flight crew and aviation ground support employees of Northwest Airlines who served overseas under the airline's

contract with Air Transport Command from Dec. 14, 1941, through Aug. 14, 1945.

28. U.S. civilian female employees of the U.S. Army Nurse Corps who served in the defense of Bataan and Corregidor during the period Jan. 2, 1942, to Feb. 3, 1945.

29. U.S. flight crew and aviation ground support employees of Northeast Airlines Atlantic Division, who served overseas as a result of Northeast Airlines' contract with the Air Transport Command during the period Dec. 7, 1941, through Aug. 14, 1945.

30. U.S. civilian flight crew and aviation ground support employees of Braniff Airways, who served overseas in the North Atlantic or under the jurisdiction of the North Atlantic Wing, Air Transport Command, as a result of a contract with the Air Transport Command during the period Feb. 26, 1942, through Aug. 14, 1945.

31. Honorably discharged members of the Alaska Territorial Guard who served during the period Dec. 31, 1941, through 1947.

Selected Reserve and National Guard: Current and former members of the Selected Reserve who served on active duty establish veteran status and may be eligible for VA benefits, depending on the length of active military service and the character of discharge. In addition, reservists not activated may qualify for some VA benefits. Members of the National Guard activated for federal service during a period of war or domestic emergency may be eligible for certain VA benefits, such as VA health care, compensation for injuries or conditions connected to that service, and burial benefits. Activation for other than federal service does not qualify guard members for all VA benefits. Claims for VA benefits based on federal service filed by members of the National Guard should include a copy of the military orders, presidential proclamation or executive order that clearly demonstrates the federal nature of the service.

Filipino Veterans: World War II era Filipino veterans are eligible for certain VA benefits. Generally, Old Philippine Scouts are eligible for VA benefits in the same manner as U.S. veterans. Commonwealth Army veterans, including certain organized Filipino guerrilla forces and New Philippine Scouts residing in the United States who are citizens or lawfully admitted for permanent residence, are also eligible for VA health care in the United States on the same basis as U.S. veterans.

Certain Commonwealth Army veterans and new Philippine Scouts may be eligible for disability compensation and burial benefits.

Other veterans of recognized guerrilla groups also might be eligible for certain VA benefits. Survivors of World War II era Filipino veterans may be eligible for dependency and indemnity compensation. Eligibility and the rates of monetary benefits may vary based on the recipient's citizenship and place of residence.

Important Documents: Those seeking a VA benefit for the first time must submit a copy of their service discharge form (DD-214, DD-215, or for WWII veterans, a WD form), which documents service dates and type of discharge, or give their full name, military service number, branch and dates of service.

The veteran's service discharge form should be kept in a safe location accessible to the veteran and next of kin or designated representative. The veteran's preference regarding burial in a national cemetery and use of a headstone provided by VA should be documented and kept with this information. The following documents will be needed for claims processing related to a veteran's death: (1) veteran's marriage certificate for claims of a surviving spouse or children; (2) veteran's death certificate if the veteran did not die in a VA health care facility; (3) children's birth certificates or adoption papers to determine children's benefits; (4) veteran's birth certificate to determine parents' benefits.

Privacy Act: The Privacy Act provides the right to access and request amendment of information collected and used by the federal government. For information, contact the Privacy Act officer at the facility where the information is maintained or visit the Privacy and Security section on VA's Home page: http://www.va.gov.

Información Para Veteranos
De Habla Hispana y Sus Dependientes

La versión en español de este folleto se encuentra disponible en formato Adobe Acrobat a través de el link (http://www.va.gov/opa/feature/index.htm) en la página de la Oficina de Asuntos Públicos del Departamento de Asuntos de Veteranos (VA) en la red mundial del internet. Las oficinas del VA en areas de gran concentración de veteranos y dependientes hispanos tienen disponibles consejeros bilingües que le pueden ayudar a aplicar para obtener beneficios. Puede encotrar una lista de las oficinas del VA en la parte de atrás de este folleto.

Health Care Benefits

Health Care Enrollment

For most veterans, entry into the VA health care system begins by applying for enrollment. Veterans do not have to be enrolled if they: (1) have a service-connected disability of 50 percent or more; (2) want care for a disability the military determined was incurred or aggravated in the line of duty, but which VA has not yet rated, during the 12-month period following discharge; or (3) want care for a service-connected disability only. To permit better planning of health resources, however, these three categories of veterans are urged to enroll.

To apply, veterans must complete VA Form 10-10EZ, Application for Health Benefits. The form may be obtained from any VA health care facility or regional benefits office, or by calling the VA Health Benefits Service Center toll-free at 1-877-222-VETS (8387). It is also available through the online applications link on VA's Home page: http://www.va.gov. Veterans may complete the form at a VA medical facility or at home and mail it to a local VA medical facility for processing. Once enrolled, eligible veterans can receive services at VA facilities anywhere in the country.

Priority Groups

Veterans will be assigned the highest priority group for which they qualify. VA uses the priority group system to balance demand with available resources. Changes in VA's available resources may reduce the number of priority groups VA can enroll. If this occurs, VA will publicize the changes and notify affected enrollees.

Veterans will be enrolled to the extent Congressional appropriations allow. If appropriations are limited, enrollment will occur based on the following priorities:

Priority Group 1: Veterans with service-connected disabilities rated 50 percent or more and veterans determined by VA to be unemployable due to service-connected conditions.

Priority Group 2: Veterans with service-connected disabilities rated 30 or 40 percent.

Priority Group 3: Veterans with service-connected disabilities rated 10 and 20 percent, veterans who are former POWs or were awarded a Purple Heart, veterans awarded special eligibility for disabilities incurred in treatment or participation in a VA Vocational Rehabilitation program, and veterans whose discharge was for a disability incurred or aggravated in the line of duty.

Priority Group 4: Veterans receiving aid and attendance or housebound benefits and veterans determined by VA to be catastrophically disabled. Some veterans in this group may be responsible for copayments.

Priority Group 5: Veterans receiving VA pension benefits or eligible for Medicaid programs, and nonservice-connected veterans and noncompensable zero percent service-connected veterans whose annual income and net worth are below the established VA means test thresholds.

Priority Group 6: Veterans of the Mexican border period or World War I; veterans seeking care solely for certain conditions associated with exposure to radiation, for any illness associated with combat service in a war after the Gulf War or during a period of hostility after Nov. 11, 1998, for any illness associated with participation in tests conducted by the Defense Department as part of Project 112/Project SHAD; and veterans with zero percent service-connected disabilities who are receiving disability compensation benefits.

Priority Group 7: Nonservice-connected veterans and noncompensable zero percent service-connected veterans with income above VA's national means test threshold and below VA's geographic means test threshold, or with income below both the VA national threshold and the VA geographically based threshold, but whose net worth exceeds VA's ceiling (currently $80,000) who agree to pay copayments.

Priority Group 8: All other nonservice-connected veterans and zero percent noncompensable service-connected veterans who agree to pay copayments. (Note: Effective Jan. 17, 2003, VA no longer enrolls new veterans in priority group 8).

Special Access to Care
Service Disabled Veterans: Veterans who are 50 percent or more disabled from service-connected conditions, unemployable due to service-connected conditions, or receiving care for a service-connected disability receive priority in scheduling of hospital or outpatient medical appointments.

Combat Veterans: Veterans who served in combat locations during active military service after Nov. 11, 1998, are eligible for free health care services for conditions potentially related to combat service for two years following separation from active duty. For additional information call 1-877-222-8387.

Financial Information

Financial Assessment
Veterans enrolling in priority group 5 based on their inability to defray the cost of care must provide information on their annual household income and net worth to determine whether they are below the annually adjusted "means test" financial threshold.

Veterans completing a financial assessment must report their annual gross household income plus net worth, which includes Social Security, U.S. Civil Service retirement, U.S. Railroad retirement, military retirement, unemployment insurance, any other retirement income, total wages from all employers, interest and dividends, workers' compensation, black lung benefits and any other gross income for the calendar year prior to application for care. Also considered are assets such as the market value of property that is not the primary residence, stocks, bonds, notes, individual retirement accounts, bank deposits, savings accounts and cash.

VA also is required to compare veterans' financial assessment information with a geographically based income threshold. If the veteran's income is below the threshold where the veteran lives, he or she is eligible for an 80-percent reduction in the inpatient copayment rates.

VA may compare income information provided by certain veterans with information obtained from the Social Security Administration and the Internal Revenue Service.

Services Requiring Copayments
Nonservice-connected veterans and noncompensable zero percent service-connected veterans whose income is above the national "means test" threshold must agree to pay appropriate copayments for care. If they do not agree to make copayments, they are ineligible for VA care.

Inpatient Care: Veterans whose income is determined to be above the means test threshold and below VA's geographically based income threshold are responsible for paying 20 percent of the Medicare deductible for the first 90 days of inpatient hospital care during any 365-day period. For each additional 90 days of hospital care, they are charged 10 percent of the Medicare deductible. In addition, the patient is charged $2 a day for hospital care. Nonservice-connected veterans and noncompensable zero percent service-connected veterans with incomes above the geographic income threshold will be charged the full Medicare deductible for the first 90 days of care during any 365-day period. For each additional 90 days, they are charged one half of the Medicare deductible and $10 per day.

Extended care: With certain exceptions, a veteran must agree to pay copayments for extended care. A veteran's application for extended care services (VAF 10-10EC) requires financial information used to determine the monthly copayment amount, based on each veteran's financial situation.

Medication: Most veterans are currently charged $7 for a 30-day or less supply of medication.

Outpatient Care: A three-tiered copayment system is effective for all outpatient services. The copayment is $15 for a primary care visit and $50 for some specialized care. Preventative care services do not require a copayment.

Outpatient Visits Not Requiring Copayments
Outpatient visits for which no copayment will be assessed include: publicly announced VA health initiatives (e.g., health fairs) or an outpatient visit solely consisting of preventive screening and/or immunizations, such as influenza immunization, pneumococcal immunization, hypertension screening, hepatitis C screening, tobacco screening, alcohol screening, hyperlipidemia screening, breast cancer screening, cervical cancer screening, screening for colorectal cancer by fecal occult blood testing, and education about the risks and

benefits of prostate cancer screening. Laboratory, flat film radiology services, and electrocardiograms are also exempt from copayments.

Billing Insurance Companies

VA is required to bill private health insurance providers for medical care and services, supplies and prescriptions provided for veterans' nonservice-connected conditions. Money collected in this way is used to maintain and improve VA's health care system. Generally, VA cannot bill Medicare for medical services provided to veterans; however, VA can bill Medicare supplemental health insurance for medical services covered by the supplemental insurance but not by Medicare.

All veterans applying for VA medical care are required to provide information on their health insurance coverage, including coverage provided under policies of their spouses. Veterans are not responsible for paying any remaining balance of VA's insurance claim that is not paid or covered by their health insurance, and any payment received by VA may be used to offset "dollar for dollar" a veteran's VA copayment responsibility.

Health Care Programs

Veteran Health Registries

VA maintains veteran health registries to provide special health examinations and health-related information to certain groups of veterans.

Gulf War Registry: For veterans who served in the Gulf War (Aug. 2, 1990, to a date not yet established) and Operation Iraqi Freedom.

Depleted Uranium Registries: VA maintains two registries for veterans possibly exposed to depleted uranium. The first is for veterans who served in the Gulf War, including Operation Iraqi Freedom. The second is for veterans who served elsewhere, including Bosnia and Afghanistan.

Agent Orange Registry: For veterans possibly exposed to dioxin or other toxic substances in herbicides used during the Vietnam War (between 1962 and 1975), while serving in Korea in 1968 or 1969, or as a result of testing, transporting, or spraying herbicides for military purposes.

Ionizing Radiation Registry: For veterans possibly exposed to atomic radiation during the following activities: participation in tests involving the atmospheric detonation of a nuclear device; occupation of Hiroshima or Nagasaki from Aug. 6, 1945, through July 1, 1946; internment as a prisoner of war in Japan during World War II; serving in official military duties at the Department of Energy gaseous diffusion plants at Paducah, Ky.; Portsmouth, Ohio; or the K-25 area at Oak Ridge, Tenn., for at least 250 days before Feb. 1, 1992, or in Longshot, Milrow or Cannikin underground nuclear tests at Amchitka Island, Alaska, before Jan. 1, 1974; or treatment with nasopharyngeal (NP) radium during military service.

Veterans eligible for participation in any VA registry may receive free, comprehensive registry medical examinations, including laboratory and other diagnostic tests deemed necessary by an examining clinician. Eligible veterans do not have to be enrolled in VA health care to participate in registry examinations. Veterans wishing to participate should contact the nearest VA health care facility or visit the Internet: http://www.va.gov/environagents/.

Readjustment Counseling Service

Readjustment counseling is provided at 206 community-based Vet Centers located in all 50 states, the District of Columbia, Guam, Puerto Rico, and the U.S. Virgin Islands, and is designed to help combat veterans in their readjustment to civilian life. Vet Center staff provide individual, group and family counseling plus a wide range of other services to include medical referral, homeless veteran services, employment services, VA benefit referral, and the brokering of non-VA services.

Eligible veterans include those who served on active duty in a combat theater during World War II, the Korean War, the Vietnam War, the Gulf War, or the campaigns in Lebanon, Grenada, Panama, Somalia, Bosnia, Kosovo, Afghanistan, Iraq and the war on terror. Veterans who served in the active military during the Vietnam Era, but not in the Republic of Vietnam, are also eligible, provided they requested services at a Vet Center before Jan. 1, 2004. Vet Centers also provide bereavement counseling to the families of military personnel killed in action and sexual trauma counseling to veterans who suffered sexual trauma while on active duty.

Readjustment difficulties can include post-traumatic stress disorder (PTSD) or any other problems that affect functioning within the family, work, school or other areas of everyday life. For additional information, contact the nearest Vet Center, listed in the federal government section of telephone directories, or visit the Internet: http://www.va.gov/rcs.

Prosthetic and Sensory Aid Services

VA will furnish needed prosthetic appliances, equipment and devices, such as artificial limbs, orthopedic braces and shoes, wheelchairs, crutches and canes, and other durable medical equipment and supplies to veterans receiving VA care for any condition. VA will provide hearing aids and eyeglasses to veterans who receive increased pension based on the need for regular aid and attendance or being permanently housebound, receive compensation for a service-connected disability or are former prisoners of war. Otherwise, hearing aids and eyeglasses will be provided only in special circumstances, and not for normally occurring hearing or vision loss. For additional information, contact the prosthetic representative at your local VA health care facility.

Services and Aids for Blind Veterans

Blind veterans may be eligible for services at a VA medical center or for admission to a VA blind rehabilitation center. Services are available at all VA medical facilities through the Visual Impairment Services coordinator. In addition, blind veterans enrolled in the VA health care system may receive VA aids for the blind, including:

1. A total health and benefits review.
2. Adjustment to blindness training.
3. Home improvements and structural alterations to homes.
4. Specially adapted housing and adaptations.
5. Automobile grant.
6. Low-vision aids and training in their use.
7. Electronic and mechanical aids for the blind, including adaptive computers and computer-assisted devices such as reading machines and electronic travel aids.
8. Guide dogs, including the expense of training the veteran to use the dog.
9. Talking books, tapes and Braille literature.

Home Improvements and Structural Alterations

VA provides funding for eligible veterans to make home improvements necessary for the continuation of treatment or for disability access to the home and essential lavatory and sanitary facilities. Home improvement benefits up to $4,100 for service-connected veterans and up to $1,200 for nonservice-connected veterans may be provided. For application information, contact the prosthetic representative at the nearest VA medical center or outpatient clinic.

Alcohol and Drug-Dependence Treatment
Veterans eligible for VA medical care may apply for substance abuse treatment. Contact the nearest VA medical facility to apply.

Compensated Work Therapy
VA provides vocational assistance and therapeutic work opportunities for eligible veterans through several programs. Each program offers rehabilitative treatment to help veterans live and work in their communities.

Incentive Therapy is a token base payment program frequently used as a precursor to Compensated Work Therapy (CWT) or as a mainstay for veterans unable to work in the community. Veterans referred to CWT receive an individualized vocational assessment, rehabilitation planning and work experience. The goal is to help veterans achieve a maximum degree of self-sufficiency based on their needs, preferences and abilities. The CWT program works closely with community-based organizations, employers and state and federal agencies to establish transitional work experiences, direct job placement and supportive follow-up services.

The CWT/Transitional Residence program provides work-based, residential treatment in a stable living environment. This program differs from other VA residential bed programs in that participants use their CWT earnings to contribute to the cost of operating and maintaining their residences and are responsible for planning, purchasing and preparing their own meals. The program offers a comprehensive array of rehabilitation services including home, financial and life skills management in a therapeutic community model.

Outpatient Dental Treatment
Outpatient dental treatment provided by VA includes examinations and the full spectrum of diagnostic, surgical, restorative and preventive procedures. Veterans eligible to receive dental care include the following: (1) veterans having service-connected and compensable dental disabilities or conditions; (2) former prisoners of war;

(3) veterans with service-connected, noncompensable dental conditions as a result of combat wounds or service injuries; (4) veterans with nonservice-connected dental conditions determined by VA to be aggravating a service-connected medical problem; (5) veterans having service-connected conditions rated as permanently and totally disabling or rated 100 percent by reason of individual unemployability; (6) veterans participating in a vocational rehabilitation program under chapter 31 of title 38; (7) certain enrolled homeless veterans participating in specific health care programs; (8) veterans with non-service connected dental conditions for which treatment was begun while the veteran was an inpatient in a VA facility when it is necessary to complete such treatment on an outpatient basis; and (9) veterans requiring treatment for dental conditions clinically determined to be complicating a medical condition currently under treatment.

Recently discharged veterans who served on active duty 90 days or more and who apply for VA dental care within 90 days of separation from active duty, may receive one time treatment for dental conditions if the veteran's certificate of discharge does not indicate that the veteran received necessary dental care within a 90-day period prior to discharge or release.

Outpatient Pharmacy Services

Outpatient pharmacy services are provided free to: (1) veterans with a service-connected disability of 50 percent or more; (2) veterans receiving medication for treatment of service-connected conditions; (3) veterans whose annual income does not exceed the maximum VA annual rate of the VA pension; (4) veterans receiving medication for conditions related to exposure to ionizing radiation; (5) veterans receiving medication for conditions related to combat service in a war after the Gulf War or against a hostile force in a period of hostilities beginning after Nov. 11, 1998; (6) veterans receiving medication for conditions related to participation in Defense Department tests conducted as part of Project 112/Project SHAD; (7) veterans receiving medication for conditions related to sexual trauma experienced while serving on active duty; (8) certain veterans receiving medication for treatment of cancer of the head or neck; (9) veterans receiving medication as part of a VA-approved research project, and (10) former prisoners of war. Other veterans will be charged a copayment of $7 for each 30-day or less supply of medication. To eliminate a financial hardship for veterans who require an unusually large amount of medications, there is a maximum copayment amount that veterans enrolled in Priority Groups 2 through 6 pay in any single year.

Veterans do not pay copayments for medications dispensed during the remainder of a calendar year in which this annual cap amount has been paid. For calendar year 2005, the cap is $840.

The medication copayment applies to prescription and over-the-counter medications, such as aspirin, cough syrup or vitamins, dispensed by a VA pharmacy. Medication copayments are not charged for medications injected during the course of treatment or for medical supplies, such as syringes or alcohol wipes. In the event over-the-counter drugs are ordered, the veteran can choose to purchase them at a local pharmacy rather than pay $7 for items such as aspirin, cough syrup or vitamins.

Nursing-Home Care

VA provides nursing home services through three national programs: VA owned and operated nursing homes, state veterans homes owned and operated by the state, and contract community nursing homes. Each program has its own admission and eligibility criteria.

VA owned and operated homes typically admit residents requiring short-term skilled care, or who have a 70 percent or more service-connected disability, or who require nursing home care because of a service-connected disability. The state veterans home program is a cooperative venture between VA and the states whereby VA provides funds to help build the home and pays a portion of the costs for veterans eligible for VA health care. The states, however, set eligibility criteria for admission. The contract nursing home program is designed to meet the long-term nursing home care needs of veterans who may not be eligible and/or qualify for placement in a VA or state veterans home or if there is no VA or state home available.

To be placed in a nursing home, veterans generally must be medically stable, have a condition that requires inpatient nursing home care, and be assessed by an appropriate medical provider to be in need of institutional nursing home care. They also must meet the eligibility requirements for the home to which they are applying. For VA nursing homes, they may have to pay a copayment depending on their financial status. VA social workers can help interpret eligibility and co-payment requirements.

In addition to nursing home care, VA offers other extended care services either directly or by contract with community agencies, including adult day care, respite care, geriatric evaluation and management, hospice and palliative care, and home based primary care. These services may require copayment.

Domiciliary Care

Domiciliary care provides rehabilitative and long-term, health-maintenance care for veterans who require minimal medical care but do not need the skilled nursing services provided in nursing homes. VA may provide domiciliary care to veterans whose annual income does not exceed the maximum annual rate of VA pension or to veterans the Secretary of Veterans Affairs determines have no adequate means of support. The copayments for extended care services apply to domiciliary care. Call your nearest benefits or health care facility for information.

Medical Care for Dependents and Survivors

CHAMPVA, the Civilian Health and Medical Program of the Department of Veterans Affairs, provides reimbursement for most medical expenses – inpatient, outpatient, mental health, prescription medication, skilled nursing care and durable medical equipment. To be eligible for CHAMPVA, an individual cannot be eligible for TRICARE (the medical program for civilian dependents provided by the Department of Defense) and must be one of the following:

1. The spouse or child of a veteran who VA has rated permanently and totally disabled for a service-connected disability.

2. The surviving spouse or child of a veteran who died from a VA-rated service-connected disability, or who, at the time of death, was rated permanently and totally disabled.

3. The surviving spouse or child of a military member who died in the line of duty, not due to misconduct. However, in most of these cases, these family members are eligible for TRICARE, not CHAMPVA.

A surviving spouse under age 55 who remarries loses CHAMPVA eligibility on midnight of the date of remarriage. However eligibility may be re-established if the remarriage is terminated by death, divorce or annulment effective the first day of the month after the termination of the remarriage or Dec. 1, 1999, whichever date is later. A CHAMPVA eligible surviving spouse who is 55 or older does not lose eligibility upon remarriage.

Individuals who have Medicare entitlement may also have CHAMPVA eligibility secondary to Medicare. Eligibility limitations apply.

For additional information or to apply for benefits, contact the VA Health Administration Center, P.O. Box 65023, Denver, CO 80206, call 1-800-733-8387 or visit the Internet: http://www.va.gov/hac/.

Many VA medical centers provide services to CHAMPVA beneficiaries under the CHAMPVA In House Treatment Initiative (CITI) program. Contact the nearest VA medical center to determine if it is a participating facility. Beneficiaries who use a CITI facility incur no cost for services they receive, however services are provided on a space available basis, after the needs of veterans are met. Therefore, not all services are available at all times. CHAMPVA beneficiaries covered by Medicare cannot use the CITI program.

Beneficiary Travel

Certain veterans may be eligible for payment or reimbursement for travel costs to receive VA medical care. Reimbursement is paid at $.11 per mile (or $.17 per mile if called for a repeat C&P exam) and is subject to a deductible of $3 for each one-way trip and an $18-per-month maximum payment. Two exceptions to the deductible are travel for a compensation or pension examination and travel by special modes of transportation, such as an ambulance or a specially equipped van. Beneficiary travel payments may be made to the following: (1) veterans whose service-connected disabilities are rated at 30 percent or more; (2) veterans traveling for treatment of a service-connected condition; (3) veterans who receive a VA pension; (4) veterans traveling for scheduled compensation or pension examinations; (5) veterans whose income does not exceed the maximum annual VA pension rate; and (6) veterans whose medical condition requires special mode of transportation, if the veteran is unable to defray the costs and travel is pre-authorized. Advance authorization is not required in a medical emergency if a delay would be hazardous to life or health.

Emergency Medical Care in Non-VA Facilities

VA may provide reimbursement or payment for medical care provided to enrolled veterans by non-VA facilities only in cases of medical emergencies where VA or other federal facilities were not feasibly available. Other conditions also apply. To determine eligibility or initiate a claim, contact the VA medical facility nearest to where the emergency service was provided.

Veterans Living or Traveling Overseas
VA will pay for medical care associated with a service-connected condition for veterans living or traveling overseas. See the Overseas Benefits section for more information.

Merchant Marine Seamen
Certain Merchant Marine seamen who served in World War II may qualify for veterans benefits. When applying for medical care, seamen must present their discharge certificate from the Department of Defense. VA regional offices can assist in obtaining a certificate.

Allied Veterans
VA is authorized to provide medical care to certain veterans of nations allied or associated with the United States during World War I or World War II. Such treatment is available at any VA medical facility if authorized and reimbursed by the foreign government. VA also is authorized to provide hospitalization, outpatient and domiciliary care to former members of the armed forces of Czechoslovakia or Poland who participated during World Wars I or II in armed conflict against an enemy of the United States, if they have been citizens of the United States for at least 10 years.

Benefit Programs

Disability Compensation

Disability compensation is a monetary benefit paid to veterans who are disabled by injury or disease incurred or aggravated during active military service. The service of the veteran must have been terminated through separation or discharge under conditions other than dishonorable. Disability compensation varies with the degree of disability and the number of dependents, and is paid monthly. The benefits are not subject to federal or state income tax. The payment of military retirement pay, disability severance pay and separation incentive payments known as SSB and VSI (Special Separation Benefits and Voluntary Separation Incentives) also affects the amount of VA compensation paid. See the "Tables" section of this booklet for more information.

Receiving Benefit Payments

VA offers three methods for receiving benefit payments. Most veterans and beneficiaries receive their payments by direct deposit through an electronic funds transfer to their bank, savings and loan or credit union accounts. In some areas, benefit recipients who do not have an account at a financial institution may open a federally insured Electronic Transfer Account, which costs about $3 a month, provides a monthly statement and allows cash withdrawals. Recipients may also choose to receive benefits by check. To choose a payment method, call VA's toll-free helpline at 1-877-838-2778, Monday through Friday, 7:30 a.m. - 4:00 p.m., Central Standard Time.

Prisoners of War

Former prisoners of war (POW) are eligible for disability compensation if they are rated at least 10 percent disabled from conditions presumed to be related to the POW experience. The following presumptive conditions apply to former POWs who were imprisoned for any length of time: psychosis, any of the anxiety states, dysthymic disorder, organic residuals of frostbite, post-traumatic osteoarthritis, heart disease (including ischemic heart disease), stroke and residuals of stroke.

Former POWs who were imprisoned for at least 30 days are also eligible for the following additional presumptive conditions: avitaminosis, beriberi, chronic dysentery, helminthiasis, malnutrition (including optic atrophy), pellagra and/or other nutritional deficiencies, irritable bowel syndrome, peptic ulcer disease, peripheral neuropathy and cirrhosis of the liver.

Agent Orange and Other Herbicides

Eleven diseases are presumed by VA to be service-related for compensation purposes for veterans exposed to Agent Orange and other herbicides used in support of military operations in the Republic of Vietnam between Jan. 9, 1962, and May 7, 1975. The diseases presumed are: chloracne or other acneform disease similar to chloracne, porphyria cutanea tarda, soft-tissue sarcoma (other than osteosarcoma, chondrosarcoma, Kaposi's sarcoma or mesothelioma), Hodgkin's disease, multiple myeloma, respiratory cancers (lung, bronchus, larynx, trachea), non-Hodgkin's lymphoma, prostate cancer, acute and subacute peripheral neuropathy, diabetes mellitus (Type 2) and chronic lymphocytic leukemia.

Veterans Exposed to Radiation

Veterans exposed to ionizing radiation while on active duty may be eligible for disability compensation if they have disabilities related to that exposure. Conditions presumed to be service-connected for veterans who participated in "radiation-risk activities" as defined by VA regulations are: all forms of leukemia (except for chronic lymphocytic leukemia); cancer of the thyroid, breast, pharynx, esophagus, stomach, small intestine, pancreas, bile ducts, gall bladder, salivary gland, urinary tract (renal pelvis, ureter, urinary bladder and urethra), brain, bone, lung, colon, and ovary, bronchiolo-alveolar carcinoma, multiple myeloma, lymphomas (other than Hodgkin's disease), and primary liver cancer (except if cirrhosis or hepatitis B is indicated). To determine service-connection for other conditions or exposures not eligible for presumptive compensation, factors considered include amount of radiation exposure, duration of exposure, elapsed time between exposure and onset of the disease, gender and family history, age at time of exposure, the extent to which a nonservice-related exposure could contribute to disease, and the relative sensitivity of exposed tissue.

Gulf War Veterans

Gulf War veterans who suffer from chronic disabilities resulting from undiagnosed illnesses, medically unexplained chronic multi-symptom illnesses (such as chronic fatigue syndrome, fibromyalgia or irritable bowel syndrome) that are defined by a cluster of signs or symptoms, and any diagnosed illness that the Secretary of Veterans Affairs determines warrants a presumption of service-connection may receive disability compensation. The undiagnosed illnesses must have appeared either during active duty in the Southwest Asia Theater of Operations during the Gulf War or to a degree of at least 10 percent at any time since then through Dec. 31, 2006.

The following symptoms are among the manifestations of an undiagnosed illness: fatigue, skin disorders, headache, muscle pain, joint pain, neurologic symptoms, neuropsychological symptoms, symptoms involving the respiratory system, sleep disturbances, gastrointestinal symptoms, cardiovascular symptoms, abnormal weight loss and menstrual disorders. A disability is considered chronic if it has existed for at least six months.

Amiotrophic Lateral Sclerosis (ALS) may also be service-connected if the veteran served in the Southwest Asia Theater of Operations during the period of Aug. 2, 1990, to July 31, 1991.

Specially Adapted Homes

Certain veterans with service-connected disabilities may be entitled to a grant from VA to assist in either building a new specially adapted home or in purchasing an existing home to modify and remodel to meet their disability-related requirements.

$50,000 Grant: VA may approve a grant of not more than 50 percent of the cost of building, buying, or adapting existing homes or paying to reduce indebtedness on a previously owned home that is being adapted, up to a maximum of $50,000. In certain instances, the full grant amount may be applied toward remodeling costs.

Veterans must be determined eligible to receive compensation for permanent and total service-connected disability due to one of the following:

    1. Loss or loss of use of both lower extremities, such as to preclude locomotion without the aid of braces, crutches, canes or a wheelchair.

    2. Loss or loss of use of both upper extremities at or above the elbow.

    3. Blindness in both eyes, having only light perception, plus loss or loss of use of one lower extremity.

    4. Loss or loss of use of one lower extremity together with (a) residuals of organic disease or injury, or (b) the loss or loss of use of

one upper extremity which so affects the functions of balance or propulsion as to preclude locomotion without the use of braces, canes, crutches or a wheelchair.

$10,000 Grant: VA may approve a grant for the actual cost, up to a maximum of $10,000, for adaptations to a veteran's residence that are determined by VA to be reasonably necessary. The grant also may be used to help veterans acquire a residence already adapted with special features for the veteran's disability. Veterans must be entitled to compensation for permanent and total service-connected disability due to (1) blindness in both eyes with 5/200 visual acuity or less, or (2) anatomical loss or loss of use of both hands.

Supplemental Financing: Veterans with available loan guaranty entitlement may also obtain a guaranteed loan or a direct loan from VA to supplement the grant to acquire a specially adapted home. Amounts with a guaranteed loan from a private lender will vary, but the maximum direct loan from VA is $33,000.

Automobile Assistance

Veterans and servicemembers qualify for this benefit if they have service-connected loss or permanent loss of use of one or both hands or feet, or permanent impairment of vision of both eyes to a certain degree. Veterans and servicemembers entitled to compensation for ankylosis (immobility) of one or both knees, or one or both hips, also qualify for adaptive equipment for an automobile. There is a one-time payment by VA of not more than $11,000 toward the purchase of an automobile or other conveyance. VA pays for adaptive equipment, and for repair, replacement, or reinstallation required because of disability, and for the safe operation of a vehicle purchased with VA assistance. To apply, contact a VA regional office at 1-800-827-1000 or the nearest VA medical center.

Clothing Allowance

Any veteran who is entitled to receive compensation for a service-connected disability for which he or she uses prosthetic or orthopedic appliances may receive an annual clothing allowance. The allowance also is available to any veteran whose service-connected skin condition requires prescribed medication that irreparably damages the veteran's outer garments. Veterans with qualifying service-connected disabilities can apply for a clothing allowance by contacting the Prosthetic and Sensory Aid Service at the closest VA health care facility.

Allowances for Dependents
Veterans whose service-connected disabilities are rated at 30 percent or more are entitled to additional allowances for dependents. The additional amount is determined by the number of dependents and the degree of disability.

Aid and Attendance or Housebound
A veteran who is determined by VA to be in need of the regular aid and attendance of another person, or a veteran who is permanently housebound, may be entitled to additional disability compensation or pension benefits. A veteran evaluated at 30 percent or more disabled is entitled to receive a special allowance for a spouse who is in need of the aid and attendance of another person.

Incarcerated Veterans
VA disability compensation and pension benefits are restricted if a veteran, surviving spouse, child or dependent parent is convicted of a felony and imprisoned for more than 60 days. The disability compensation paid to an incarcerated veteran is limited to the 10 percent disability rate. For a surviving spouse, child, dependent parent or veteran whose disability rating is 10 percent, the payment is reduced by one half. Any amounts not paid may be apportioned to eligible dependents. Payments are not reduced for recipients participating in work-release programs, residing in halfway houses or under community control. Overpayments for failure to notify VA of a veteran's incarceration result in the loss of all financial benefits until the overpayment is recovered.

Fugitive Felons
VA disability compensation and pension benefits may not be paid to any veteran named on an outstanding felony warrant, or their dependents, until the veteran has surrendered to authorities or the warrant is cleared.

Pension
Veterans with low incomes who are permanently and totally disabled, or are age 65 and older, may be eligible for monetary support if they have 90 days or more of active military service, at least one day of which was during a period of war. Generally, veterans who entered active duty on or after Sept. 8, 1980, or officers who entered active duty on or after Oct. 16, 1981, may have to meet a longer minimum

period of active duty. The discharge from active duty must have been under conditions other than dishonorable. The permanent and total disability must be for reasons other than the veteran's own willful misconduct. Payments are made to qualified veterans to bring their total income, including other retirement or Social Security income, to a level set by Congress. Unreimbursed medical expenses may reduce countable income. Veterans of a period of war who are age 65 or older and meet service and income requirements are also eligible to receive a pension, regardless of current physical condition.

Improved Pension
The Improved Pension program provides for the maximum annual rates listed in the "Tables" section of this booklet. The payment is reduced by the amount of the countable income of the veteran and the income of the spouse or dependent children. When a veteran without a spouse or a child is furnished nursing-home or domiciliary care by VA, the pension is reduced to an amount not to exceed $90 per month after three calendar months of care. The reduction may be delayed if nursing-home care is being continued for the primary purpose of providing the veteran with rehabilitation services.

Protected Pension Programs
Beneficiaries of Old-Law or Section 306 pension who do not wish to elect Improved Pension can continue to receive the pension rate they were receiving on Dec. 31, 1978. This rate generally continues as long as income remains within established limits, net worth does not bar payment, and beneficiaries do not lose dependents. Beneficiaries must continue to meet basic eligibility factors, such as permanent and total disability for veterans, or status as a surviving spouse or child. VA also must adjust rates for other reasons, such as a veteran's hospitalization in a VA facility.

Medal of Honor Pension
VA administers pensions to holders of the Medal of Honor. Congress set the monthly pension at $1,027 effective Dec. 1, 2004.

Vocational Rehabilitation and Employment

Vocational Rehabilitation and Employment is an employment-oriented program that helps veterans with service-connected disabilities prepare for, find and keep suitable employment.

Suitable employment is work that is within a veterans' physical, mental and emotional capabilities and matches their patterns of skills, talents and interests. For veterans whose disabilities are so severe they cannot currently consider employment, VA helps them attain as much independence in daily living as possible. Additional information is available on the Internet: http://www.vba.va.gov.

Eligibility

A veteran must have a VA established service-connected disability rated 10 percent disabling with a serious employment handicap or at least 20 percent with an employment handicap and be discharged or released from military service under other than dishonorable conditions. A servicemember pending medical separation from active duty may apply, but the disability rating must be at least 20 percent.

Services

Depending on an individual's needs, services provided by VA may include:

    1. An evaluation of the individual's talents, skills and interests.
    2. Employment services such as job-seeking skills, resume development and other work readiness assistance.
    3. Assistance getting and keeping suitable employment.
    4. Vocational counseling and planning.
    5. Training, such as on-the-job and work experience programs.
    6. Training, such as certificate, two, or four-year college or technical programs.
    7. Supportive rehabilitation services and additional counseling.

VA pays the cost of these services and pays a living allowance to veterans who participate in training.

Entitlement

Eligible veterans are evaluated to determine if they need vocational rehabilitation services to help overcome barriers to employment.

Period of a Rehabilitation Program

Generally, veterans must complete a vocational rehabilitation program within 12 years from their separation from military service or within 12 years from the date VA notifies them that they have a compensable service-connected disability. Depending on the length of program needed, veterans may be provided up to 48 months of full-time services or their part-time equivalent. These limitations may be extended in certain circumstances.

Work-Study
Participants may be paid a work-study allowance if they train at the three-quarter or full-time rate. They may elect to be paid in advance a portion of the allowance equal to 40 percent of the total. Participants under the supervision of a VA employee may provide VA outreach services, prepare and process VA paperwork, and work at a VA medical facility or perform other VA-approved activities.

Children of Vietnam Veterans Born with Certain Birth Defects

Children of Vietnam veterans born with certain birth defects may be eligible for benefits under one of two separate programs—the Spina Bifida Program or the Children of Women Vietnam Veterans Program. Benefits under both programs include a monthly monetary allowance, health care specific to the disability, and vocational training if reasonably feasible. The law defines "child" as the natural child of a Vietnam veteran, regardless of age or marital status. The child must have been conceived after the date on which the veteran first entered the Republic of Vietnam. Qualifying service includes active military, naval or air service, including service in the waters offshore and other locations if the service involved duty or visitation in Vietnam. Questions about either program may be sent via e-mail to: birthdefect@vba.va.gov.

Spina Bifida Program
This program applies to biological children of male and female veterans who served in Vietnam during the period beginning Jan. 9, 1962, and ending May 7, 1975, or who served in or near the Korean demilitarized zone (DMZ) during the period beginning Sept. 1, 1967, and ending Aug. 31, 1971. A monetary allowance is paid at three disability levels based on the neurological manifestations that define the severity of disability: impairment of the functioning of extremities, impairment of bowel or bladder function, and impairment of intellectual functioning.

Children of Women Vietnam Veterans Program

This program applies to biological children of women veterans who served in Vietnam during the period beginning on Feb. 28, 1961, and ending on May 7, 1975. The birth defects covered are those that are associated with a mother's service in Vietnam and that resulted in a permanent physical or mental disability. The covered birth defects do not include conditions due to familial disorders, birth-related injuries, or fetal or neonatal infirmities with well-established causes. A monetary allowance is paid at four disability levels based on the child's degree of permanent disability.

Allowances

The 2005 monthly rates for both programs can be found in the "Tables" section of this booklet. Contact a VA regional office to apply for medical treatment or benefits payments. Note: a monetary allowance paid to an individual under these programs shall not be considered as income or resources in determining eligibility for, or the amount of benefits paid under, any other federal or federally assisted program.

Vocational Training

The Vocational Rehabilitation and Employment Program administers a vocational training program to enable a qualified child to prepare for and attain suitable employment. Services may include counseling and rehabilitative services, education, training and employment services leading to suitable employment. VA pays for these services.

To qualify for a vocational training program, an applicant must be a child:
    1. To whom VA has awarded a monthly allowance for spina bifida, or for whom VA has established the existence of another covered birth defect, and
    2. For whom VA has determined that achievement of a vocational goal is reasonably feasible.

A vocational training program may not begin before a child's 18th birthday or the date the child completes secondary schooling, whichever comes first. Depending on need and eligibility for VA education benefits, a child may be provided up to 48 months of full-time training.

Education and Training

Education laws are complex. The following is only a summary. Additional information for school officials, veterans and dependents can be found on the Internet at: http://www.gibill.va.gov or by calling 1-888-GI-BILL-1 (1-888-442-4551).

Montgomery GI Bill

Eligibility

The Montgomery GI Bill (MGIB) provides education benefits that may be used while on active duty or after separation from active duty. Veterans must receive a fully honorable military discharge for the period of service on which MGIB eligibility is based. Discharges "under honorable conditions" and "general" discharges do not establish eligibility. Veterans who do not receive a qualifying discharge from one period of service may qualify based on a discharge from another qualifying period of service.

All participants must have a high school diploma or equivalency certificate before applying for benefits. Completing 12 hours toward a college degree before applying for benefits also meets this requirement. Under previous law, veterans were required to meet the high school requirement before they completed their initial active duty obligation. Those who did not may now meet the requirement and apply or reapply for benefits. If eligible, they must use their benefits within the following period: (1) 10 years from the date of last discharge from active duty, or (2) by Nov. 2, 2010, whichever is later.

Additionally, every veteran must establish eligibility under one of the following four categories.

Category 1 – Service After June 30, 1985

To be eligible under Category 1, veterans must: have entered active duty for the first time after June 30, 1985, and not have declined MGIB in writing upon entry on to active duty. The military reduces their pay $100 a month for 12 months of active duty. These pay reductions are not refundable. Eligible servicemembers can use the MGIB benefit while on active duty after completing two continuous years of service. Veterans can use the MGIB benefit if they: completed three continuous years of active duty, or two continuous years of active duty if they first signed up for less than three years or have an obligation to serve four years in the Selected Reserve (the 2x4 program) and enter the Selected Reserve within one year of release from active duty.

Servicemembers or veterans are barred from eligibility under Category 1, however, if they received a commission as a result of graduation from a service academy or completion of an ROTC scholarship. However, such a commission isn't a bar if the applicant: (1) received a commission after becoming eligible for MGIB benefits (including completing the minimum service requirements for the initial period of active duty); or (2) received a commission after Sept. 30, 1996, and received less than $3,400 during any one year under ROTC scholarship.

Under Category 1, applicants are also barred from benefits if they declined MGIB because they received repayment from the military for education loans. If they did not decline MGIB and received loan repayments, the months served to repay the loans will be deducted from MGIB entitlement. Individuals who received loan repayments for one period of active duty can still be eligible based on another qualifying period of active duty as long as they did not decline MGIB upon entering active duty.

Early Separation
Veterans who did not complete the required period of service may still be eligible under Category 1 if discharged for one of the following reasons: (1) convenience of the government—with 30 continuous months of service for an obligation of three or more years, or 20 continuous months of service for an obligation of less than three years; (2) service-connected disability; (3) hardship; (4) a medical condition diagnosed prior to joining the service; (5) a condition that interfered with performance of duty and didn't result from misconduct; (6) a reduction in force (in most cases). Servicemembers planning to separate early should ensure their separation reasons are coded properly to avoid disqualification for MGIB benefits.

Category 2 – Vietnam Era GI Bill Conversion
To be eligible under Category 2, veterans must have had remaining entitlement under the Vietnam Era GI Bill on Dec. 31, 1989. Additionally, they must have served on active duty for any number of days during the period Oct. 19, 1984, to June 30, 1985, and served on active duty for at least three continuous years beginning on July 1, 1985; or at least two continuous years active duty beginning

on July 1, 1985, followed by a minimum of four years in the Selected Reserve beginning within one year of release from active duty.

Veterans not on active duty on Oct. 19, 1984, may be eligible under Category 2 if they served three continuous years on active duty at any time beginning on or after July 1, 1985, or two continuous years of active duty at any time followed by four continuous years in the Selected Reserve beginning within one year of release from active duty.

Veterans are barred from eligibility under Category 2 if they received a commission after Dec. 31, 1976, as a result of graduation from a service academy or completion of an ROTC scholarship. However, such a commission isn't a bar if they received the commission after becoming eligible for MGIB benefits, or received the commission after Sept. 30, 1996, and received less that $3,400 during any one year under ROTC scholarship.

Category 3 – Involuntary Separation/Special Separation
Veterans may be eligible under Category 3 if they meet one of the following requirements: (1) elected MGIB before being involuntarily separated; or (2) were voluntarily separated under the Voluntary Separation Incentive or the Special Separation Benefit program, elected MGIB benefits before being separated, and had military pay reduced by $1,200 before discharge.

Category 4 – Veterans Educational Assistance Program
Eligibility under Category 4 may be extended to veterans who participated in the Veterans Educational Assistance Program (VEAP) if they: (1) served on active duty on Oct. 9, 1996; (2) participated in VEAP and contributed money to a VEAP account; (3) elected MGIB by Oct. 9, 1997, and paid $1,200. Veterans who participated in VEAP on or before Oct. 9, 1996, may also be eligible even if they did not deposit money in a VEAP account if they served on active duty from Oct. 9, 1996, through April 1, 2000, elected MGIB by Oct. 31, 2001, and contributed $2,700 to MGIB.

Certain National Guard servicemembers may also qualify under Category 4 if they: (1) served for the first time on full-time active duty in the National Guard under title 32, U.S.C., between June 30, 1985, and Nov. 29, 1989, and had no previous active duty service; (2) elected MGIB during the nine-month window ending on July 9, 1997; and (3) paid $1,200.

Period of Eligibility
Eligibility generally expires 10 years after discharge or release from active duty. However, there are exceptions for disability, re-entering active duty, and upgraded discharges.

Payments
For training in college, technical or vocational school, eligible veterans qualify to receive the following monthly rates for full-time training effective Oct. 1, 2004: $1,004 a month if they qualify for MGIB benefits based on active duty for three continuous years or more or active duty for two continuous years plus four years in the Selected Reserve, or $816 a month if they qualify for MGIB benefits based on active duty of less than three years. Benefits are reduced for part-time training. Payments for other types of training follow different rules. For complete tables of current benefit rates, visit: http://www.gibill.va.gov.

VA will pay an additional amount, commonly called a "kicker" or "college fund" if directed by the Department of Defense. Eligibility is based on occupational specialties and is generally established upon the servicemember's recruitment into active duty. Servicemembers potentially eligible under Category 1 (or originally eligible under Category 1 but subsequently eligible under Category 3 because of the reason for discharge) can make additional contributions up to $600 before leaving active duty to receive a higher rate of benefits.

The maximum number of months veterans can receive MGIB benefits is 36 months at the full-time rate or the part-time equivalent. The following groups qualify for the maximum: (1) eligible veterans who served the required length of active duty, (2) eligible veterans with an obligation of three years or more who were separated early for the convenience of the government and served 30 continuous months, (3) eligible veterans with an obligation of less than three years who were separated early for the convenience of the government and served 20 continuous months.

Training Available
The following types of training are available under the Montgomery GI Bill: (1) courses at colleges and universities leading to associate, bachelor or graduate degrees, including accredited independent study, which may be offered through distance education; (2) courses leading to a certificate or diploma from business, technical or vocational schools; (3) apprenticeship or on-the-job training programs for

individuals not on active duty, including self-employment training begun on or after June 16, 2004, necessary for ownership or operation of a franchise; (4) correspondence courses, under certain conditions; (5) flight training, if the veteran holds a private pilot's license upon beginning the training program and meets the medical requirements; (6) state-approved teacher certification programs; (7) preparatory courses necessary for admission to a college or graduate school; (8) licensing and certification tests approved for veterans; and (9) entrepreneurship training courses to create or expand small businesses.

Additional MGIB Benefits
1. Accelerated payment of MGIB benefits is available to those enrolled in certain high-cost programs leading to employment in the technology industry.
2. Transfer of entitlement to dependents is provided by the U.S. Air Force in limited circumstances.
3. Tutorial assistance allowance is available for individual tutoring if training in school at one-half time or more. The maximum benefit is $1,200 ($100 per month).
4. Tuition Assistance Top-Up provides for payment to an individual for the difference between the tuition assistance amount paid by the military component and the total cost of tuition and approved charges.

Work-Study
Veterans may be eligible for a work-study program in which they work for VA and receive hourly wages. Veterans must train at the three-quarter or full-time rate. The types of work allowed include:
(1) outreach services for VA and State Approving Agencies;
(2) VA paperwork; (3) work at national or state veterans' cemeteries;
(4) work at VA medical centers or state veterans homes; and
(5) other VA approved activities.

Counseling
VA counseling is available to help MGIB participants assess their educational and vocational strengths and weaknesses. Counseling is also available to help plan education or employment goals. Additionally, individuals not eligible for the MGIB may still receive VA counseling beginning 180 days prior to separation from active duty through the first full year following honorable discharge.

Montgomery GI Bill – Selected Reserve

Eligibility
The Montgomery GI Bill – Selected Reserve provides education benefits to members of the reserve elements of the Army, Navy, Air Force, Marine Corps and Coast Guard, and to members of the Army National Guard and the Air National Guard. To be eligible for this program, a reservist must: (1) incur a six-year obligation to serve in the Selected Reserve signed after June 30, 1985, or, if an officer, agree to serve six years in addition to the original obligation; (2) complete Initial Active Duty for Training; (3) have a high school diploma or equivalency certificate before applying for benefits; and (4) remain in good standing in a Selected Reserve unit.

Reserve components determine eligibility for benefits. VA does not make decisions about eligibility and cannot make payments until the reserve component has determined eligibility and notified VA.

Period of Eligibility
If a reservist separates from the Selected Reserve, benefits generally end the day of separation. If an individual stays in the Selected Reserve, benefits generally end 14 years from the date the reservist became eligible for the program. For reservists who became eligible before Oct. 1, 1992, benefits generally end 10 years from the date they became eligible. Under special circumstances, eligibility may be extended.

Payments
The full-time rate effective Oct. 1, 2004, is $288 a month for 36 months for full-time training. Part-time benefits are reduced proportionately. For complete current rates, visit: http://www.gibill.va.gov. The Department of Defense may make additional contributions, or "kickers," on behalf of individuals in critical military fields, as deemed necessary to encourage enlistment.

Training Available
Eligible reservists may take undergraduate or technical training at colleges and universities. Those who have a six-year commitment beginning after Sept. 30, 1990, may also take the following training: graduate courses, courses for a certificate or diploma from business, technical or vocational schools; cooperative training; apprenticeship or on-the-job training; correspondence courses; independent study programs; flight training; entrepreneurship training, or remedial, deficiency or refresher courses needed to complete a program of study.

Work-Study
Eligibility for the Work-Study program under the Selected Reserve Montgomery GI Bill is the same as in the Montgomery GI Bill.

Tutorial Assistance
Benefits for tutorial assistance are the same as in the regular Montgomery GI Bill.

Counseling
VA counseling is available to help participants assess their educational and vocational strengths and weaknesses. Counseling is also available to help plan educational or employment goals.

Veterans' Educational Assistance Program (VEAP)

Eligibility
Under VEAP, active duty personnel voluntarily participated in a plan for education or training in which their savings were administered and added to by the federal government. Servicemembers were eligible to enroll in VEAP if they entered active duty for the first time after Dec. 31, 1976, and before July 1, 1985. Some contribution to VEAP must have been made prior to April 1, 1987. The maximum participant contribution is $2,700. While on active duty, participants may make a lump-sum contribution to their VEAP account.

Servicemembers who participated in VEAP are eligible to receive benefits while on active duty if: (1) at least three months of contributions are available, except for high school or elementary school, in which case only one month is needed; and (2) they enlisted for the first time after Sept. 7, 1980, and completed 24 months of their first period of active duty. Visit http://www.gibill.va.gov for length of service requirements for those who enlisted for the first time prior to Sept. 7, 1980.

To use benefits after separation from active duty, veterans must receive a discharge under conditions other than dishonorable for the qualifying period of service.

Veterans who enlisted for the first time after Sept. 7, 1980, or entered active duty as an officer or enlistee after Oct. 16, 1981, must have completed 24 continuous months of active duty, unless they meet a qualifying exception.

Period of Eligibility
Eligibility generally expires 10 years from the date of last discharge or release from active duty. Under special circumstances, the 10-year period may be extended.

Payments
The Department of Defense will match the participant's contribution at the rate of $2 for every $1 the individual put into the fund. The Department of Defense may make additional contributions, or "kickers," on behalf of individuals in critical military fields, as deemed necessary to encourage enlistment. For training in college, vocational or technical schools, the amount of money participants receive each month depends on the type and hours of training pursued. The maximum basic rate is $300 a month for full-time training.

Training Available
VEAP participants may pursue: associate, bachelor or graduate degrees at colleges or universities including accredited independent study, which may be offered through distant education; courses leading to a certificate or diploma from business, technical or vocational schools; apprenticeship or on-the-job training programs; cooperative courses which consist of a full-time program of alternating school instruction and training in business or industry; correspondence courses; flight training; tutorial assistance; refresher, remedial or deficiency courses if needed to complete a program of study; refresher training to update skills for technological advances that occurred while the veteran was on active duty or after separation; and state-approved alternative teacher certification programs. VEAP participants may also receive benefits for approved licensing and certification tests, and for entrepreneurship training.

Work-Study
Eligibility for the Work-Study program under VEAP is the same as under the Montgomery GI Bill.

Tutorial Assistance
Benefits for tutorial assistance are the same as under the Montgomery GI Bill.

Counseling
Eligibility for VA counseling under VEAP is the same as under the Montgomery GI Bill.

Home Loan Guaranties

VA loan guaranties are made to servicemembers, veterans, reservists and unmarried surviving spouses for the purchase of homes, condominiums and manufactured homes, and for refinancing loans. VA guarantees part of the total loan, permitting the purchaser to obtain a mortgage with a competitive interest rate, even without a down payment if the lender agrees. VA requires that a down payment be made for the purchase of a manufactured home. VA also requires a down payment for a home or condominium if the purchase price exceeds the reasonable value of the property or the loan has a graduated payment feature. With a VA guaranty, the lender is protected against loss up to the amount of the guaranty if the borrower fails to repay the loan. A VA loan guaranty can be used to:

1. Buy a home.
2. Buy a residential condominium.
3. Build a home.
4. Repair, alter or improve a home.
5. Refinance an existing home loan.
6. Buy a manufactured home with or without a lot.
7. Buy and improve a manufactured home lot.
8. Install a solar heating or cooling system or other weatherization improvements.
9. Purchase and improve a home simultaneously with energy-efficient improvements.
10. Refinance an existing VA loan to reduce the interest rate and make energy-efficient improvements.
11. Refinance a manufactured home loan to acquire a lot.

Eligibility
Applicants must have a good credit rating, have an income sufficient to support mortgage payments, and agree to live in the property.
To obtain a VA Certificate of Eligibility, complete VA Form 26-1880, Request for a Certificate of Eligibility for VA Home Loan Benefits, and mail it to one of the two VA Eligibility Centers (Winston-Salem, N.C., and Los Angeles). In general, those veterans living in the Western part of the country mail their applications to the Los Angeles Eligibility Center, while those living in the Eastern part of the country mail applications to Winston-Salem. Additional information on eligibility and addresses for the Centers is available on VA's loan guaranty eligibility Home page: http://www.homeloans.va.gov/elig.htm. Veterans may also have their lenders obtain a Certificate of Eligibility for them

through VA's ACE (Automated Certificate of Eligibility) system. This is an online application that, in some cases, can generate a certificate immediately. Not all cases can be processed through this system but, if all necessary information is available, ACE provides the quickest way to determine eligibility.

Periods of Eligibility

World War II: (1) active duty service after Sept. 15, 1940, and prior to July 26, 1947; (2) discharge under other than dishonorable conditions; and (3) at least 90 days service unless discharged early for a service-connected disability.

Post-World War II: (1) active duty service after July 25, 1947, and prior to June 27, 1950; (2) discharge under other than dishonorable conditions; and (3) 181 days continuous active duty unless discharged early for service-connected disability.

Korean War: (1) active duty after June 26, 1950, and prior to Feb. 1, 1955; (2) discharge under other than dishonorable conditions; and (3) at least 90 days total service, unless discharged early for a service-connected disability.

Post-Korean War: (1) active duty between Jan. 31, 1955, and Aug. 5, 1964; (2) discharge under conditions other than dishonorable; (3) 181 days continuous service, unless discharged early for service-connected disability.

Vietnam: (1) active duty after Aug. 4, 1964, and prior to May 8, 1975; (2) discharge under conditions other than dishonorable; and (3) 90 days total service, unless discharged early for service-connected disability. For veterans who served in the Republic of Vietnam, the beginning date is Feb. 28, 1961.

Post-Vietnam: For veterans whose enlisted service began before Sept. 8, 1980, or whose service as an officer began before Oct. 17, 1981: (1) active duty for 181 continuous days, all of which occurred after May 7, 1975, and discharge under conditions other than dishonorable or early discharge for service-connected disability.

24-Month Rule: If service was between Sept. 8, 1980, (Oct. 16, 1981, for officers) and Aug. 1, 1990, veterans must generally complete 24 months of continuous active duty or the full period (at least 181 days) for which they were called or ordered to active duty, and be discharged under conditions other than dishonorable. Exceptions are allowed if the veteran completed at least 181 days of active duty but was discharged earlier than 24 months for (1) hardship, (2) the convenience of the government, (3) reduction-in-force, (4) certain medical conditions, or (5) service-connected disability.

Gulf War: Veterans of the Gulf War era, which began Aug. 2, 1990, and will continue until Congress or the President declares it has ended, must generally complete 24 months of continuous active duty or the full period (at least 90 days) for which they were called or ordered to active duty, and be discharged under conditions other than dishonorable. Exceptions are allowed if the veteran completed at least 90 days of active duty but was discharged earlier than 24 months for (1) hardship, (2) the convenience of the government, (3) reduction-in-force, (4) certain medical conditions, or (5) service-connected disability.

Reservists and National Guard members are eligible if they were activated after Aug. 1, 1990, served at least 90 days, and received an honorable discharge.

Active Duty Personnel: Until the Gulf War era is ended by law or Presidential Proclamation, persons on active duty are eligible after serving on continuous active duty for 90 days.

Members of the Selected Reserve: Individuals are eligible if they have completed at least six years of honorable service in the reserves or National Guard or were discharged because of a service-connected disability. Reservists who do not qualify for VA housing loan benefits may be eligible for loans on favorable terms insured by the Federal Housing Administration (FHA) of the Department of Housing and Urban Development (HUD).

Others: Other eligible individuals include unmarried spouses of veterans or reservists who died on active duty or as a result of service-connected causes; surviving spouses who remarry after attaining age 57; spouses of active-duty servicemembers who have been missing in action or a prisoner of war for at least 90 days; U.S. citizens who served in the armed forces of a U.S. ally in World War II; and members of organizations with recognized contributions to the U.S. World War II effort. Eligibility may be determined at the VA Eligibility Centers.

Guaranty Amount

The guaranty amount is the amount of the VA guaranty available to an eligible veteran and may be considered the equivalent of a down payment by lenders. The basic VA guaranty amount is $36,000. The maximum guaranty amount for purchase or construction loans in excess of $144,000 is equal to 25 percent of the Freddie Mac conforming loan limit determined under section 305(a)(2) of the Federal Home Loan Mortgage Corporation Act for a single family residence. The amount of entitlement varies with the loan amount. Loan guaranty limits are listed in the "Tables" section of this booklet.

VA does not establish a maximum loan amount. However, no loan for the acquisition of a home may exceed the reasonable value of the property, which is based on an appraiser's estimate. A buyer, seller, real estate agent or lender can request a VA appraisal by completing VA Form 26-1805, Request for Determination of Reasonable Value. The requester pays for the appraisal, often called a "VA appraisal," according to a fee schedule approved by VA. This VA appraisal estimates the value of the property, but is not an inspection and does not guarantee that the house is free of defects. VA guarantees the loan, not the condition of the property.

A loan for the purpose of refinancing existing mortgage loans or other liens secured on a dwelling is generally limited to 90 percent of the appraised value of the dwelling. A loan to reduce the interest rate on an existing VA-guaranteed loan, however, can be made for an amount equal to the outstanding balance on the old loan plus closing costs, up to two discount points, and energy-efficient improvements. A loan for the purchase of a manufactured home or lot is limited to 95 percent of the amount that would be subject to finance charges. The VA funding fee and up to $6,000 in energy-efficient improvements also may be included in the loan.

A veteran who previously obtained a VA loan can use the remaining entitlement for a second purchase. The amount of remaining entitlement is the difference between $36,000 (25 percent of certain loans as previously described) and the amount of entitlement used on prior loans. Remaining entitlement is not necessary for veterans to refinance an existing VA loan with a new one at a lower interest rate.

Required Occupancy

Veterans must certify that they intend to live in the home they are buying or building with a VA guaranty. A veteran who wishes to refinance or improve a home with a VA guaranty also must certify to being in occupancy at the time of application. A spouse may certify occupancy if the buyer is on active duty. In refinancing a VA-guaranteed loan solely to reduce the interest rate, veterans need only certify to prior occupancy.

Closing Costs
Payment in cash is required on all home loan closing costs, including title search and recording, hazard insurance premiums, prepaid taxes and a one percent origination fee, which may be required by lenders in lieu of certain other costs. In the case of refinancing loans, all such costs may be included in the loan, as long as the total loan does not exceed 90 percent of the reasonable value of the property. Interest Rate Reduction Refinancing Loans may include closing costs and a maximum of two discount points. Loans, including refinancing loans, are charged a funding fee by VA, except for loans made to disabled veterans and unmarried surviving spouses of veterans who died as a result of service. The VA funding fee is based on the loan amount and, at the discretion of the veteran and the lender, may be included in the loan. Funding fee rates are listed in the "Tables" section of this booklet.

Financing, Interest Rates and Terms
Veterans obtain VA-guaranteed loans through the usual lending institutions, including banks, savings and loan associations, building and loan associations, and mortgage loan companies. Veterans may obtain a loan with a fixed interest rate, which may be negotiated with the lender. Veterans also may obtain an Adjustable Rate Mortgage (ARM) where the interest rate can be adjusted up to one percent annually and up to five percent over the life of the loan. Veterans may choose a hybrid ARM where the initial interest rate remains fixed for three to ten years. If the rate remains fixed for less than five years, the rate adjustment cannot be more than one percent annually and five percent over the life of the loan. For a hybrid ARM with an initial fixed period of five years or more, the initial adjustment may be up to two percent. Adjustments thereafter are limited to one percent annually and six percent over the life of the loan.

If the lender charges discount points on the loan, the veteran may negotiate with the seller as to who will pay points or if they will be split between buyer and seller. Points paid by the veteran may not be included in the loan, except that a maximum of two points may be included in Interest Rate Reduction Refinancing Loans. The loan may be for as long as 30 years and 32 days.

VA does not require that a down payment be made, except in the following instances: (1) a manufactured home or lot loan; (2) a loan with graduated payment features; and (3) to prevent the amount of a loan from exceeding VA's determination of the property's reasonable value. If the sale price exceeds the reasonable value, the veteran must certify that the difference is being paid in cash without supplementary borrowing. A cash down payment of five percent of the purchase price is required for manufactured home or lot loans.

Release of Liability, Loan Assumption

When a veteran sells a home financed through a VA guaranty to a purchaser who assumes the loan, the veteran may request release from liability to the federal government, provided the loan is current, the purchaser has been obligated by contract to purchase the property and assume all of the veteran's liabilities, and VA is satisfied that the purchaser is a good risk. A release of liability does not mean that a veteran's guaranty entitlement is restored. If the new veteran-buyer agrees to substitute entitlement for that of the veteran-seller, entitlement may be restored to the veteran-seller.

A VA loan for which a commitment was made on or after March 1, 1988, is not assumable without approval of VA or its authorized agent. The person who assumes a VA loan for which a commitment was made on or after that date must pay a fee to VA. If a person disposes of the property securing a VA-guaranteed loan for which a commitment was made after March 1, 1988, without first notifying the holder of the loan, the holder may demand immediate and full payment of the loan. Veterans whose loans were closed after Dec. 31, 1989, have no liability to the government following a foreclosure, except in cases involving fraud, misrepresentation or bad faith.

Loans for Native American Veterans

VA direct home loans are available to eligible Native American veterans who wish to purchase, construct or improve a home on Native American trust land. These loans may be used to simultaneously purchase and improve a home. Direct loans also are available to reduce the interest rate on existing loans obtained under this program. VA direct loans may be limited to the cost of the home or $80,000, whichever is less. A funding fee must be paid to VA. The fee is 1.25 percent for loans to purchase, construct or improve a home. For loans to refinance an existing loan, the fee is 0.5 percent of the loan amount. Veterans receiving compensation for service-connected disability are not required to pay the funding fee. The funding fee may be paid in cash or included in the loan. The following may not be included in the loan: VA appraisal, credit report, loan processing fee, title search, title insurance, recording fees, transfer taxes, survey charges or hazard insurance.

Repossessed Homes
VA acquires properties as a result of foreclosures on VA guaranteed loans. These properties are marketed through a property management services contract with Ocwen Federal Bank, and listed by local agents through the Multi-Listings System. A listing of properties for sale may be obtained on the Internet: http://www.ocwen.com. Contact a real estate agent for information on purchasing a VA acquired property.

Safeguards for Veterans
The following home loan guaranty safeguards have been established to protect veterans:

1. Homes completed less than a year before purchase with VA financing and inspected during construction by either VA or HUD must meet VA requirements.
2. VA may suspend from the loan program those who take unfair advantage of veteran borrowers or decline to sell a new home or make a loan because of race, color, religion, sex, disability, family status or national origin.
3. The builder of a new home is required to give the purchasing veteran a one-year warranty that the home has been constructed to VA-approved plans and specifications. A similar warranty must be given for new manufactured homes.
4. In cases of new construction completed under VA or HUD inspection, VA may pay or otherwise compensate a veteran borrower for correction of structural defects seriously affecting livability if assistance is requested within four years of a home loan guaranty.
5. The borrower obtaining a loan may only be charged the fees and other charges prescribed by VA as allowable.
6. The borrower can prepay without penalty the entire loan or any part not less than the amount of one installment or $100.
7. VA encourages holders to extend forbearance if a borrower becomes temporarily unable to meet the terms of the loan.

Life Insurance

There are currently eight VA life insurance programs. Only four of these programs are currently open to new issues. Two of those open to new issues, the Service-Disabled Veterans Insurance and Veterans' Mortgage Life Insurance programs, are specifically designed for disabled veterans. The other two "open" programs, Servicemembers' Group Life Insurance (SGLI) and Veterans' Group Life Insurance (VGLI), are administered by the Office of Servicemembers' Group Life Insurance (290 W. Mt. Pleasant Ave., Livingston, NJ 07039-2747, phone 1-800-419-1473) under the supervision of VA.

Servicemembers' Group Life Insurance

The following are automatically insured for $250,000 under SGLI: active-duty members of the Army, Navy, Air Force, Marines and Coast Guard; commissioned members of the National Oceanic and Atmospheric Administration and the Public Health Service; cadets or midshipmen of the service academies; members, cadets and midshipmen of the ROTC while engaged in authorized training; members of the Ready Reserves; and members who volunteer for assignment to a mobilization category in the Individual Ready Reserve or Inactive National Guard. Individuals may elect to be covered for a lesser amount or not to be covered at all. Part-time coverage may be provided to members of the reserves who do not qualify for full-time coverage. Premiums are deducted automatically from an individual's pay or are collected by the individual's service branch. At the time of separation from service, SGLI can be converted to either VGLI or a commercial permanent plan through participating companies. SGLI coverage continues for 120 days after separation at no charge.

Family Servicemembers' Group Life Insurance

Family Servicemembers' Group Life Insurance (FSGLI) is essentially a rider to SGLI. It provides up to $100,000 of life insurance coverage for spouses, not to exceed the amount of SGLI the insured member has in force, and automatically provides $10,000 for dependent children of members insured under the SGLI program with no premium required. FSGLI is a servicemembers' benefit, and the member pays the premium and is the beneficiary of the policy. If a servicemember drops his or her SGLI coverage or leaves the military, the spouse's policy can be converted to a private life insurance policy within 120 days of the date the servicemember's SGLI coverage ended.

Veterans' Group Life Insurance

SGLI may be converted to Veterans' Group Life Insurance (VGLI), which provides renewable five-year term coverage. VGLI is available to: (a) individuals with full-time SGLI coverage upon release from active duty or the reserves; (b) individuals with part-time SGLI coverage who incur a disability or aggravate a pre-existing disability during a reserve period which renders them uninsurable at standard premium rates; and (c) members of the Individual Ready Reserve and Inactive National Guard.

Individuals who separate from service with SGLI coverage can convert to VGLI by submitting an application and the initial premium within 120 days of separating. After 120 days, the individual may still be granted VGLI provided an application, initial premium and evidence of insurability are submitted within one year of termination of SGLI coverage. Servicemembers who are totally disabled at the time of separation are eligible for the SGLI Disability Extension of up to one year. The extension of coverage is free and continues for one year from separation or until the veteran is no longer disabled, whichever comes first. In cases where SGLI coverage is continued under the SGLI Disability Extension provision, VGLI coverage will automatically be issued at the end of the SGLI coverage period subject only to the payment of premiums. VGLI is convertible at any time to a permanent plan policy with any of the commercial insurance companies that participate in the program.

Accelerated Death Benefits for SGLI, FSGLI and VGLI

A member insured under SGLI or VGLI, if terminally ill (prognosis of nine months or less to live), may elect to receive up to 50 percent of the coverage amount in advance. Servicemembers with FSGLI coverage may also elect to receive up to 50 percent of their spouse's coverage if the spouse becomes terminally ill.

Service-Disabled Veterans Insurance

A veteran who was discharged from service under other than dishonorable conditions and who has a service-connected disability but is otherwise in good health may apply to VA for up to $10,000 in life insurance coverage within two years from the date of the award of service connection. This insurance is limited to veterans who left service on or after April 24, 1951. Veterans who are totally disabled may apply for a waiver of premiums. For those veterans who are eligible for this waiver, additional supplemental coverage of up to $20,000 is available. However, premiums cannot be waived on the additional insurance. To be eligible for this type of supplemental insurance, veterans must meet all of the following four requirements: (1) have an RH policy, (2) be under age 65, (3) meet the requirements for total disability, and (4) apply for this additional insurance within one year from the date of notification of having met total disability requirements.

Veterans' Mortgage Life Insurance
VMLI is available to severely disabled veterans who have been approved for a Specially Adapted Housing Grant. Maximum coverage is $90,000, and is only payable to the mortgage company. Protection is issued automatically provided the veteran submits information required to establish a premium and does not decline coverage. Coverage automatically terminates when the mortgage is satisfied. If a mortgage is disposed of through sale of the property, VMLI may be obtained on the mortgage of another home.

Insurance Dividends
Active government life insurance policies beginning with the letters V, RS, W, J, JR, JS or K automatically pay dividends annually on the policy anniversary date. Policyholders do not need to apply for these dividends, but may select from a number of options for how they should be handled. VA insurance dividends, and interest on dividends left on deposit or credit with VA, are not taxable. For more information, visit the VA Life Insurance Program Web page: http://www.insurance.va.gov or contact the VA Insurance Center at 1-800-669-8477. Many policyholders may access their own policy information online at the VA Insurance Web site above.

Policyholders with National Service Life Insurance, Veterans Special Life Insurance and Veterans Reopened Insurance can use their dividends to purchase additional paid-up coverage only at the time the dividend is issued.

Persistent rumors about special SGLI or VGLI dividends and dividends for holders of lapsed policies are not true.

Miscellaneous Insurance Information
Reinstating Lapsed Insurance: Lapsed term policies may be reinstated within five years from the date of lapse. Contact the VA Insurance Center for details. A five-year term policy that is not lapsed at the end of the term period is automatically renewed for an additional five-year period. Lapsed permanent plan policies may be reinstated within certain time limits and with certain health requirements. Reinstated policies require repayment of all back premiums, plus interest.

Converting Term Policies: A term policy that is in force may be converted to a permanent plan. Upon reaching renewal at age 70 or older, National Service Life Insurance term policies on total disability premium waiver are automatically converted to permanent insurance, which provides cash and loan values and higher dividends.

Paid-up Insurance Available on Term Policies: Effective September 2000, VA provides paid-up insurance on term policies whose premiums have been capped. Prior to this date, reserves were not available on terminated term policies. Veterans who have NSLI term insurance (renewal age 71 or older) and decide to stop paying premiums on their policies will be given a termination dividend. This dividend will be used to purchase a reduced amount of paid-up insurance, which insures the veteran for life and no premium payments are required. The amount of insurance remains level.

Disability Provisions: National Service Life Insurance policyholders who become totally disabled before age 65 should consult VA about premium waivers.

Borrowing on Policies: Policyholders may borrow up to 94 percent of the cash surrender value of their insurance. Interest on policy loans is compounded annually. The current interest rate may be obtained by calling toll-free 1-800-669-8477.

For additional information about government life insurance, visit the VA Internet site: http://www.insurance.va.gov or call toll-free 1-800-669-8477. Specialists are available between the hours of 8:30 a.m. and 6 p.m., Eastern Time, to discuss premium payments, insurance dividends, address changes, policy loans, naming beneficiaries and reporting the death of the insured. After hours, a caller may leave a recorded message, which will be answered on the next workday, or may use the Interactive Voice Response system.

If the insurance policy number is not known, send whatever information is available, such as the veteran's VA file number, date of birth, Social Security number, military serial number or military service branch and dates of service to:

>Department of Veterans Affairs
>Regional Office and Insurance Center
>Box 42954
>Philadelphia, PA 19101

Burial Benefits

Eligibility

Veterans discharged under conditions other than dishonorable and servicemembers who die while on active duty may be eligible for the following burial benefits: (1) burial in a national cemetery; (2) government-furnished headstone or marker; (3) Presidential Memorial Certificate; (4) burial flag; and in some cases, (5) reimbursement of a portion of burial expenses. With certain exceptions, service beginning after Sept. 7, 1980, as an enlisted person, and after Oct. 16, 1981, as an officer, must be for a minimum of 24 consecutive months or the full period for which the person was called to active duty. Reservists and National Guard members are eligible if they were entitled to retired pay at the time of death, or would have been entitled had they not been under the age of 60.

Certain Filipino veterans of World War II, to include those who served in the Philippine Commonwealth Army (USAFFE) or recognized guerilla forces and New Philippine Scouts, may be eligible if the veteran, at the time of death, was a citizen of the United States or an alien lawfully admitted for permanent residence in the United States.

Persons convicted of a federal or state capital crime, and sentenced to death or life imprisonment without parole, are barred from receiving burial benefits. For additional information on burial benefits, call the nearest national cemetery or 1-800-827-1000, or visit: http://www.cem.va.gov/.

Burial in VA National Cemeteries

VA provides veterans and dependents several gravesite options for burial, though choices are limited to those available at a specific cemetery. These may include a full casket burial, or columbarium or in-ground niche for cremated remains. A limited number of national cemeteries also provide a scatter garden for cremated remains.

The funeral director or the next of kin makes interment arrangements for an eligible veteran or dependent at the time of need by contacting the national cemetery in which burial is desired. VA normally does not conduct burials on weekends. However, weekend callers will be directed to a national cemetery that can schedule burials for the following week. Gravesites in national cemeteries cannot be reserved, however VA will honor reservations made under previous programs.

See the VA Facilities section of this book to locate a national cemetery.

Spouses and dependent children of eligible veterans and servicemembers also may be buried in a national cemetery. If the surviving spouse of an eligible veteran remarries, and that marriage is terminated by death or dissolved by annulment or divorce, the surviving spouse is eligible for burial in a national cemetery. The surviving spouse need not be unmarried at the time of death to retain eligibility, if the date of death is on or after Jan.1, 2000. Burial of dependent children is limited to unmarried children under 21 years of age, or under 23 years of age if pursuing a full-time course of instruction at an approved educational institution. Unmarried adult children who became physically or mentally disabled and incapable of self-support before reaching the age of 21, or 23 if a full-time student, also are eligible for burial.

Headstones and Markers

Flat bronze, granite or marble markers and upright granite or marble headstones are available. In national cemeteries, the style chosen must be consistent with existing monuments at the place of burial. Niche markers are available to mark columbaria used for inurnment of cremated remains. Government-furnished headstones and markers must be inscribed with the name of the deceased, branch of service, and the year of birth and death. They also may be inscribed with other markings, including an authorized emblem of belief and, space permitting, additional text including military grade, rate or rank; war service such as "World War II;" complete dates of birth and death; military awards; military organizations; civilian or veteran affiliations; and words of endearment. When burial or memorialization is in a national, state or military veterans cemetery, the headstone or marker must be ordered through cemetery officials. To apply or obtain specific information on available styles, contact the cemetery where the headstone or marker is to be placed.

When burial occurs in a private cemetery, an application for a government-furnished headstone or marker must be made to VA. The government will ship the headstone or marker free of charge, but will not pay for its placement. Headstones and markers previously provided by the government may be replaced at government expense if badly deteriorated, illegible, vandalized or stolen. Eligible veterans and servicemembers buried in private cemeteries, whose deaths occurred on or after Sept. 11, 2001, may receive a government-furnished headstone or marker regardless of whether the grave is already marked with a non-government memorial.

To apply, mail a completed VA Form 40-1330, Application for Standard Government Headstone or Marker for Installation in a Private or State Veterans Cemetery, along with a copy of the veteran's military service discharge document to Memorial Programs Service (402E), Department of Veterans Affairs, 810 Vermont Avenue, NW, Washington, DC, 20420-0001. Or fax documents to 1-800-455-7143. Do not send original discharge documents because they will not be returned. For information and application instructions, visit: http://www.cem.va.gov.

VA also provides memorial headstones and markers, bearing the inscription "In Memory of" as their first line, to memorialize eligible veterans and servicemembers whose remains were not recovered or identified, were buried at sea, donated to science or cremated and scattered. Eligible dependents may be memorialized only in national or state veterans cemeteries. To be memorialized, dependents do not need to outlive the veteran from whom their eligibility is based. Memorial headstones or markers must be placed in national, state veterans, local or private cemeteries. VA supplies and ships memorial headstones and markers free of charge, but does not pay for their plots or placement. To check the status of an application for headstone or marker, call 1-800-697-6947.

Presidential Memorial Certificates

Certificates signed by the president are issued upon request to recognize the military service of honorably discharged deceased veterans. Next of kin, other relatives and friends may request them in person at any VA regional office or by mail: Presidential Memorial Certificates, Department of Veterans Affairs, 5109 Russell Rd., Quantico, VA 22143-3909. There is no pre-printed form to complete or time limit for requesting a certificate(s), but requests should include a copy, not the original, of the deceased veteran's discharge document and clearly indicate to what address the certificate(s) should be sent. Additional information and a sample certificate can be found on the Internet: http://www.cem.va.gov/pmc.htm.

Burial Flags

VA will furnish a United States burial flag for memorialization of:
  (1) Veterans who served during wartime, or served after Jan. 31, 1955.

(2) Veterans who were entitled to retired pay for service in the reserves, or would have been entitled to such pay but not for being under 60 years of age.

(3) Members or former members of the Selected Reserve who served at least one enlistment or, in the case of an officer, the period of initial obligation, or were discharged for disability incurred or aggravated in line of duty, or died while a member of the Selected Reserve.

Reimbursement of Burial Expenses

VA will pay a burial allowance up to $2,000 if the veteran's death is service-connected. In some instances, VA also will pay the cost of transporting the remains of a service-disabled veteran to the national cemetery nearest the home of the deceased that has available gravesites. In such cases, the person who bore the veteran's burial expenses may claim reimbursement from VA. There is no time limit for filing reimbursement claims in service-connected death cases.

VA will pay a $300 burial and funeral expense allowance for veterans who, at time of death, were entitled to receive pension or compensation or would have been entitled to compensation but for receipt of military retirement pay. Eligibility also may be established when death occurs in a VA facility, a nursing home under VA contract or a state veterans nursing home. Additional costs of transportation of the remains may be paid. In nonservice-connected death cases, claims must be filed within two years after permanent burial or cremation.

VA will pay a $300 plot allowance when a veteran is not buried in a cemetery that is under U.S. government jurisdiction under the following circumstances: the veteran was discharged from active duty because of disability incurred or aggravated in the line of duty; the veteran was in receipt of compensation or pension or would have been except for receiving military retired pay; or the veteran died in a VA facility.

The $300 plot allowance may be paid to the state if a veteran is buried without charge for the cost of a plot or interment in a state-owned cemetery reserved solely for veteran burials. Burial expenses paid by the deceased's employer or a state agency will not be reimbursed.

Military Funeral Honors

Upon request, the Department of Defense will provide military funeral honors for the burial of military members and eligible veterans.

A basic military funeral honors ceremony consists of the folding and presentation of the United States flag and the playing of Taps by a bugler, if available, or by electronic recording. A funeral honors detail to perform this ceremony consists of two or more uniformed members of the armed forces, with at least one member from the service in which the deceased veteran served.

The Department of Defense maintains a toll-free telephone line (1-877-MIL-HONR) for use by funeral directors only to request honors. Family members should inform their funeral directors if they desire military funeral honors for a veteran. VA national cemetery staff can help arrange for honors during burials at VA national cemeteries. Veterans service organizations or volunteer groups may help provide honors. For more information, visit the military funeral honors Web page: http://www.militaryfuneralhonors.osd.mil.

Veterans' Cemeteries Administered by Other Agencies

Arlington National Cemetery: The Department of the Army administers Arlington National Cemetery. Eligibility for burial is more restrictive than at VA national cemeteries. Information may be found on the Internet http://www.arlingtoncemetery.org/ or by writing to Superintendent, Arlington National Cemetery, Arlington, VA 22211, or calling 703-607-8585.

Department of the Interior: The Department of the Interior administers two active national cemeteries: Andersonville National Cemetery in Georgia and Andrew Johnson National Cemetery in Tennessee. Eligibility for burial is similar to VA cemetery eligibility.

State Veterans Cemeteries: Individual states operate cemeteries for veterans. Eligibility requirements may differ from those for national cemeteries. Contact the state cemetery or state veterans affairs office for additional information. To locate a state veterans cemetery, visit the Internet: http://www.cem.va.gov/lsvc.htm.

Survivor Benefits

Dependency and Indemnity Compensation (DIC)
Dependency and Indemnity Compensation (DIC) may be available for surviving spouses who have not remarried, surviving spouses who remarry after attaining age 57, unmarried children under 18, helpless children, those between 18 and 23 if attending a VA-approved school, and low-income parents of deceased servicemembers or veterans. For survivors to be eligible, the deceased veteran must have died from: (1) a disease or injury incurred or aggravated while on active duty or active duty for training; (2) an injury incurred or aggravated in line of duty while on inactive duty training; or (3) a disability compensable by VA. Death cannot be the result of the veteran's willful misconduct. If a spouse remarries, eligibility for benefits may be restored if the marriage is terminated later by death, annulment or divorce.

DIC also may be authorized for survivors of veterans who at the time of death, were determined to be totally disabled as a result of military service, even though their service-connected disabilities did not cause their deaths. The survivor qualifies if: (1) the veteran was continuously rated totally disabled for a period of 10 or more years immediately preceding death; (2) the veteran was so rated for a period of at least five years from the date of military discharge; or (3) the veteran was a former prisoner of war who died after Sept. 30, 1999, and who was continuously rated totally disabled for a period of at least one year immediately preceding death. Payments are subject to offset by any amount received from judicial proceedings brought on account of the veteran's death. The discharge must have been under conditions other than dishonorable.

DIC Payments to Surviving Spouse
Surviving spouses of veterans who died on or after Jan. 1, 1993, receive $993 a month. For a spouse entitled to DIC based on the veteran's death prior to Jan. 1, 1993, the amount paid is $993 or an amount based on the veteran's pay grade. See the "Tables" section of this booklet for more information.

In addition to the basic rate, $250 per month is payable to a surviving spouse who has a minor child or children. This benefit is payable for the initial two years of entitlement to DIC or until the last minor child is removed from the benefit, if earlier than two years. This transitional benefit is payable for all original DIC awards commencing on or after Jan. 1, 2005. Surviving spouses awarded DIC from Feb. 1, 2003, through Dec. 31, 2004, are entitled to that portion of the two-year period that remains as of Jan. 1, 2005.

DIC Payments to Parents and Children
The monthly payment for parents of deceased veterans depends upon their income. There are additional DIC payments for dependent children. A child may be eligible if there is no surviving spouse, and the child is unmarried and under age 18, or if the child is between the ages of 18 and 23 and attending school. See the "Tables" section of this booklet for more information on DIC for children.

Special Allowances
Surviving spouses and parents receiving DIC may be granted a special allowance to pay for aid and attendance of another person if they are patients in a nursing home or require the regular assistance of another person. Surviving spouses receiving DIC may be granted a special allowance if they are permanently housebound. Current allowances are listed in the "Tables" section of this booklet.

Restored Entitlement Program for Survivors
Survivors of veterans who died of service-connected causes incurred or aggravated prior to Aug. 13, 1981, may be eligible for a special benefit. This benefit is similar to the benefit for students and surviving spouses with children between ages 16 and 18 that was eliminated from the Social Security benefit program. The benefit is payable in addition to any other benefits to which the family may be entitled. The amount of the benefit is based on information provided by the Social Security Administration.

Death Pension
Pension based on need is available for surviving spouses and unmarried children of deceased veterans with wartime service. Spouses must not have remarried and children must be under age 18, or under age 23 if attending a VA-approved school. Pension is not payable to those with estates large enough to provide maintenance. The veteran must have been discharged under conditions other than dishonorable and must have had 90 days or more of active military service, at least one day of which was during a period of war, or a service-connected disability justifying discharge for disability. If the veteran died in service but not in the line of duty, pension may be payable if the veteran had completed at least two years of honorable service. Children who become incapable of self-support because of

a disability before age 18 may be eligible for a pension as long as the condition exists, unless the child marries or the child's income exceeds the applicable limit. A surviving spouse may be entitled to higher income limitations or additional benefits if living in a nursing home, in need of the aid and attendance of another person or permanently housebound.

The Improved Pension Program provides a monthly payment to bring an eligible person's income to a support level established by law. The payment is reduced by the annual income from other sources such as Social Security paid to the surviving spouse or dependent children. Medical expenses may be deducted from the income ceiling. Pension is not payable to those who have assets that can be used to provide adequate maintenance. Maximum rates for the Improved Death Pension are shown in the "Tables" section of this booklet.

Home Loan Guaranties

A VA loan guaranty to acquire a home may be available to an unmarried spouse of a veteran or servicemember who died as a result of service-connected disabilities, a surviving spouse who remarries after attaining age 57, or to a spouse of a servicemember who has been officially listed as missing in action or as a prisoner of war for more than 90 days. Spouses of those listed as prisoners of war or missing in action are limited to one loan.

Dependents Educational Assistance

Dependents Educational Assistance benefits are available to spouses who have not remarried and children of: (1) veterans who died or are permanently and totally disabled as the result of a disability arising from active military service; (2) veterans who died from any cause while rated permanently and totally disabled from service-connected disability; (3) servicemembers listed for more than 90 days as currently missing in action or captured in line of duty by a hostile force; (4) servicemembers listed for more than 90 days as currently detained or interned by a foreign government or power.

The termination of a surviving spouse's remarriage — either by death or divorce — will reinstate Dependents' Educational Assistance benefits to the surviving spouse. If a surviving spouse ceases living with another person who has been held out publicly as the person's spouse, there is no bar to granting Dependents Educational Assistance benefits to the surviving spouse.

Benefits may be awarded for pursuit of associate, bachelor or graduate degrees at colleges and universities, including independent study, cooperative training and study abroad programs. Courses leading to a certificate or diploma from business, technical or vocational schools also may be taken.

Benefits may be awarded for apprenticeships, on-the-job training programs and farm cooperative courses. Benefits for correspondence courses under certain conditions are available to spouses only. Secondary-school programs may be pursued if the individual is not a high-school graduate. An individual with a deficiency in a subject may receive tutorial assistance benefits if enrolled halftime or more. Deficiency, refresher and other training also may be available.

Monthly Payments
Payments are made monthly. The rate effective Oct. 1, 2004, is $803 a month for full-time school attendance, with lesser amounts for part-time training. A person may receive educational assistance for full-time training for up to 45 months or the equivalent in part-time training. Payments to a spouse end 10 years from the date the individual is found eligible or from the date of the death of the veteran. VA may grant an extension. Children generally must be between the ages of 18 and 26 to receive education benefits, though extensions may be granted.

Work-Study
Participants in the work-study program must train at the three-quarter or full-time rate. They may be paid in advance 40 percent of the amount specified in the work-study agreement or an amount equal to 50 times the applicable hourly minimum wage, whichever is less. Under the supervision of a VA employee, participants may provide outreach services, prepare and process VA paperwork, work at a VA medical facility, or perform other approved activities. They also may help at national or state veterans' cemeteries or assist in outreach services furnished by State Approving Agencies.

Counseling Services
VA may provide counseling services to help an eligible dependent pursue an educational or vocational objective.

Special Benefits
An eligible child over age 14 with a physical or mental disability that impairs pursuit of an educational program may receive special restorative training to lessen or overcome that impairment. This

training may include speech and voice correction, language retraining, lip reading, auditory training, Braille reading and writing, and similar programs. Certain disabled or surviving spouses are also eligible for special restorative training. Specialized vocational training also is available to an eligible spouse or child over age 14 who is handicapped by a physical or mental disability that prevents pursuit of an educational program.

Montgomery GI Bill Death Benefit
VA will pay a special Montgomery GI Bill death benefit to a designated survivor in the event of the service-connected death of an individual while on active duty or within one year after discharge or release. The deceased must either have been entitled to educational assistance under the Montgomery GI Bill program or a participant in the program who would have been so entitled but for the high school diploma or length-of-service requirement. The amount paid will be equal to the participant's actual military pay reduction, less any education benefits paid.

Women Veterans

Women veterans are eligible for the same VA benefits as male veterans. However, additional gender-specific services and benefits are available for women veterans, including breast and pelvic examinations and other general reproductive health care services. VA provides preventive health care counseling, contraceptive services, menopause management, Pap smears and mammography. Referrals are made for services that VA is unable to provide. Women Veterans' Program Managers are available in a private setting at all VA facilities to assist women veterans seeking treatment and benefits.

VA health care professionals provide counseling and treatment to help veterans overcome psychological trauma resulting from sexual trauma that occurred while serving on active duty. Appropriate care and services are provided for any injury, illness or psychological condition resulting from such trauma.

Homeless Veterans

A number of VA benefits, including disability compensation, pension and education benefits, can prevent at-risk veterans from becoming homeless. VA conducts community-based "stand downs" to make benefits information and assistance more accessible to homeless veterans. Homeless veterans also are provided special assistance through other VA program initiatives.

VA provides health and rehabilitation programs for eligible homeless veterans. Health Care for Homeless Veterans programs provide outreach and comprehensive medical, psychological and rehabilitation treatment programs. Domiciliary Care for Homeless Veterans programs provide residential rehabilitation services. VA supports Compensated Work Therapy/Therapeutic Residence group homes, special daytime, drop-in centers, and Comprehensive Homeless Centers.

VA's Homeless Providers Grant and Per Diem Program assists nonprofit and local government agencies to establish housing or service centers for homeless veterans. Grants are awarded for the construction, acquisition or renovation of facilities. VA also works with the Department of Housing and Urban Development, the Social Security Administration, veterans service organizations, and community nonprofit groups to assist homeless veterans. For information on benefits for homeless veterans, contact the nearest VA facility. More information about this program, including information about VA loan guarantees for construction or rehabilitation of multifamily transitional housing for homeless veterans, can be found on the Internet at: http://www.va.gov/homeless/.

The Homeless Veterans' Reintegration Program (HVRP), sponsored by the Dept. of Labor's Veterans Employment and Training Service (VETS), focuses on the provision of employment and training services for homeless veterans to enable their successful reintegration into the workforce. Organizations receiving HVRP grants, including faith-based organizations, typically provide job search, counseling, job placement assistance, remedial education, classroom and on-the-job training. A list of current HVRP grantees is located on the Internet: http://www.dol.gov/vets/grants/main.htm. For additional information, contact VETS: http://www.dol.gov/vets/aboutvets/contacts/main.htm or call 202-693-4700.

Overseas Benefits

Medical Benefits
VA will pay for medical services for the treatment of service-connected disabilities and related conditions or for medical services needed as part of a vocational rehabilitation program for veterans living or traveling outside the United States. Before using the program, veterans living in the Philippines should register with the U.S. VA office in Pasay City, phone 011-632-833-4566. All other veterans living or planning to travel outside the U.S. should register with the Denver Foreign Medical Program office, P.O. Box 65021, Denver, CO 80206-9021, USA, phone 303-331-7590. Veterans living or traveling in Germany, Panama, Australia, Italy, United Kingdom, Japan and Spain can call toll free 877-345-8179. Veterans in Mexico or Costa Rico can use the same number but must first dial the United States country code.

Other Overseas Benefits
VA monetary benefits, including compensation, pension, educational assistance and burial allowances, generally are payable overseas. Some programs in foreign jurisdictions are restricted. Home-loan guaranties are available only in the United States and selected U.S. territories and possessions. Educational benefits are limited to approved degree-granting programs in institutions of higher learning. Beneficiaries residing in foreign countries should contact the nearest American embassy or consulate for information and claims assistance. In Canada, veterans should contact an office of Veterans Affairs Canada. Additional information on benefits and services available outside the United States can be found on the Internet: (http://www.vba.va.gov/bln/21/foreign/index.htm).

Small and Disadvantaged Businesses

VA's Office of Small and Disadvantaged Business Utilization helps small businesses obtain information on acquisition opportunities with VA. Like other federal offices, VA is required to place a portion of its contracts and purchases with small and disadvantaged businesses. For information, write the U.S. Department of Veterans Affairs (OOSB), 810 Vermont Avenue, N.W., Washington, D.C. 20420-0001, call toll-free 1-800-949-8387 or visit: http://www.va.gov/osdbu.

The Center for Veterans Enterprise (CVE) helps veterans interested in forming or expanding small businesses. The CVE helps VA contracting offices identify veteran-owned small businesses and works with the Small Business Administration's Veterans Business Development Officers and Small Business Development Centers nationwide regarding veterans' business financing, management and technical assistance needs. For more information, write the U.S. Department of Veterans Affairs (OOVE), 810 Vermont Avenue, N.W., Washington, D.C. 20420-0001, call toll-free1-866-584-2344 or visit the Web site: http://www.vetbiz.gov.

Appeals

Veterans and other claimants for VA benefits have the right to appeal decisions made by a VA regional office or medical center. Typical issues appealed are disability compensation, pension, education benefits, recovery of overpayments, and reimbursement for medical services that were not authorized.

A claimant has one year from the date of the notification of a VA decision to file an appeal. The first step in the appeal process is for a claimant to file a written notice of disagreement with the VA regional office or medical center that made the decision. This is a written statement that a claimant disagrees with VA's decision. Following receipt of the written notice, VA will furnish the claimant a "Statement of the Case" describing what facts, laws and regulations were used in deciding the case. To complete the request for appeal, the claimant must file a "Substantive Appeal" within 60 days of the mailing of the Statement of the Case, or within one year from the date VA mailed its decision, whichever period ends later.

Board of Veterans' Appeals

The Board of Veterans' Appeals, located in Washington, D.C., makes decisions on appeals on behalf of the Secretary of Veterans Affairs. Although it is not required, a veterans service organization, an agent or an attorney may represent a claimant. Appellants may present their case in person to a member of the Board at a hearing in Washington, D.C., at a VA regional office or by videoconference.

The texts of appeal decisions made by the Board, as well as a plain-language pamphlet, "Understanding the Appeal Process," can be found on the Internet: http://www.va.gov/vbs/bva. This pamphlet may also be requested by writing to Hearings and Transcription Unit (0141A), Board of Veterans' Appeals, 810 Vermont Avenue, NW, Washington, DC 20420.

U.S. Court of Appeals for Veterans Claims

A final Board of Veterans' Appeals decision that does not grant a claimant the benefits desired may be appealed to the U.S. Court of Appeals for Veterans Claims, an independent court, not part of the Department of Veterans Affairs.

Notice of an appeal must be received by the court with a postmark that is within 120 days after the date — stamped on the decision — on which the Board of Veterans' Appeals mailed its decision. The court reviews the record considered by the Board of Veterans' Appeals. It does not hold trials or receive new evidence. Appellants may represent themselves before the court or have lawyers or approved agents as representatives. Oral argument is held only at the direction of the court. Either party may appeal a decision of the court to the U.S. Court of Appeals for the Federal Circuit and may seek review in the Supreme Court of the United States.

The court's Web site (http://www.vetapp.gov) contains its published decisions, case status information, rules and procedures, and other special announcements. The court's decisions can also be found in West's Veterans Appeals Reporter, and on the Westlaw and LEXIS online services. For other questions, write to the Clerk of the Court, 625 Indiana Ave. NW, Suite 900, Washington, DC 20004, or call the clerk's office at 202-501-5970.

Workplace Benefits

Some benefits for veterans and their dependents are administered by agencies other than the Department of Veterans Affairs. The following information describes these benefits and how to apply for them.

Unemployment Compensation

Weekly unemployment compensation may be paid to discharged servicemembers for a limited period of time. The amount and duration of payments are determined by individual states. To apply, veterans who do not begin civilian employment immediately after leaving military service should contact their nearest state employment office and present a copy of their military discharge, Form DD-214.

Transition Assistance Program

The Transition Assistance Program is available to servicemembers and their spouses who are scheduled for separation from active duty. The program, a joint effort by the Departments of Defense, Labor, Homeland Security and Veterans Affairs, provides employment and training information to servicemembers within 12 months of their separation or 24 months of retirement from the military. Together with the military services, these agencies offer a number of services to help separating servicemembers learn basic job-hunting skills and gain the self-confidence necessary to make informed career choices.

Three-day workshops to help separating servicemembers and their spouses begin the transition from military to civilian employment are conducted at military installations. Additional information is available through the Veterans Employment and Training Service staff in each state. Addresses and phone numbers are listed in the government section of telephone directories under Department of Labor and on the Internet: http://www.dol.gov/vets/aboutvets/contacts/main.htm.

Pre-separation Counseling

The military services are required by law to provide individual pre-separation counseling at least 90 days prior to servicemember's discharge. These sessions present information on education, training, employment assistance, National Guard and reserve programs, medical benefits and financial assistance to separating service members.

Verification of Military Experience and Training
The Verification of Military Experience and Training (VMET) Document, DD Form 2586, helps servicemembers verify previous experience and training to potential employers, write their resumes, prepare for job interviews, negotiate credits at schools, and obtain certificates or licenses. VMET documents are available only through Army, Navy, Air Force and Marine Corps Transition Support offices and are intended for separating or retiring servicemembers who have at least six months of active duty service. Servicemembers should obtain VMET documents from their Transition Support office within 12 months of separation or 24 months of retirement.

Transition Bulletin Board (TBB)
Veterans may find employment opportunities on the TBB Web site: http://www.dmdc.osd.mil/ot. The site contains business opportunities, a calendar of transition seminars, job fairs, information on military and veterans associations, transition services, training and educational opportunities, as well as other announcements pertinent to separating personnel.

DoD Transportal
DoD supplements the various transition assistance resources available to separating military personnel through the Web site: http://www.dodtransportal.org. In addition to providing the locations and phone numbers of all Transition Assistance Offices, the site offers mini-courses on conducting successful job search campaigns, writing resumes, using the Internet to find a job and links to job search and recruiting Web sites. Additional resources may be found on the Internet: http://www.dod.jobsearch.org features.

Veterans' Workforce Investment Program
This program seeks to increase employment, job retention, earnings, and occupational skills of recently separated veterans and veterans who have service-connected disabilities, significant barriers to employment or who served on active duty in the armed forces during a campaign or expedition for which a campaign badge was authorized. These programs may be conducted through state or local public agencies, community-based organizations or private, nonprofit organizations. Job counseling, resume preparation, job development and placement services are also available to help homeless veterans re-enter the workforce. Veterans should contact the nearest state employment service office for more information.

State Employment Services

In addition to providing unemployment compensation information, Workforce Career or One-Stop Centers provide a variety of services for veterans seeking employment, including current employment information, education and training opportunities, job counseling and job search workshops and resume preparation assistance. Disabled Veterans Outreach Program specialists at these offices and at VA regional offices and Vet Centers work closely with employers, veterans service organizations, community-based organizations and other government agencies to promote job development and improve employment and training opportunities for disabled veterans. Local Veterans Employment Representatives are also available to provide specialized services in each state. For additional information, visit: http://www.dol.gov/vets/programs/fact/Employment_Services_fs01.htm.

Re-employment Rights

A person who left a civilian job to enter active duty in the armed forces may be entitled to return to the job after discharge or release from active duty. Re-employment rights are provided for those who served in the active duty or reserve components of the armed forces. To be re-employed, four requirements must be met: (1) the person must give advance notice of military service to the employer; (2) the cumulative absence from the civilian job shall not exceed five years (with some exceptions); (3) the person must submit a timely application for re-employment; and (4) the person must not have been released with a dishonorable or other punitive discharge.

The law calls for the returning veteran to be placed in the job as if the veteran had remained continuously employed. This means that the person may be entitled to benefits that are based on seniority, such as pensions, pay increases and promotions. The law also prohibits discrimination in hiring, promotion or other advantages of employment on the basis of military service. Applications for re-employment should be given, verbally or in writing, to a person authorized to represent the company for hiring purposes. A record should be kept of the application. If there are problems gaining re-employment, the employee should contact the Department of Labor's Veterans' Employment and Training Service (VETS) in the state of the employer concerned. This applies to private sector, as well as state, local and federal government employees, including the Postal Service. Employees should contact their agency personnel office if they have questions about their employment restoration rights. If a veteran is not re-employed or is not re-employed properly, the veteran has the right to file a complaint with VETS. Additionally, federal employees may appeal directly to the Merit Systems Protection Board. Non-federal employees may file complaints in U.S. District Court. Additional information is available on the Internet from the Department of Labor at: http://www.dol.gov/vets/welcome.html.

Federal Jobs for Veterans

Certain veterans, principally those who are disabled or who served in a hostile area, are entitled to preference for civil service jobs being filled by open, competitive exams. This preference includes five or 10 points added to passing scores in examinations and preference in job retention. Preference also is provided for certain unremarried widows and widowers of deceased veterans and for mothers of military personnel who died in service; spouses of service-connected disabled veterans who are no longer able to work in their usual occupations; and mothers of veterans who have permanent and total service-connected disabilities. Individuals interested in federal employment should contact the personnel offices of the federal agencies in which they wish to be employed. Visit the Office of Personnel Management (OPM) Web site: http://www.usajobs.opm.gov for information on creating a federal resume or to post a resume online.

Veterans enjoy many advantages in applying for federal jobs, but they are not guaranteed a position. Federal agencies are required by law to adhere to Merit System Principles in making appointments. Agencies have broad authority under law to select from a number of different sources of candidates. An agency can, for example, hire from an open competitive list of eligibles in which case veterans' preference applies.

Alternatively, the agency can reinstate a former federal employee, transfer someone from another agency, reassign someone from within the agency, make a selection under merit promotion procedures, or appoint someone noncompetitively who is eligible under a special appointing authority such as a Veterans Readjustment Appointment or the special authority for 30 percent or more disabled veterans. Veterans' preference is not a factor here, and the decision of which authority to use rests solely with the agency.

Finally, veterans who are eligible under the more recent Veterans' Employment Opportunities Act enjoy the right to apply for jobs under agency merit promotion procedures that are closed to others outside the federal service. However, veterans receive no preference under this authority.

Veterans Readjustment Appointment (VRA)
VRA allows federal agencies to appoint eligible veterans to jobs without competition. Such appointments may lead to conversion to career or career-conditional employment upon satisfactory work for two years. Veterans seeking VRA appointment should apply directly to the agency where they wish to work. OPM administers the Disabled Veterans Affirmative Action Program, which requires that all federal departments and agencies establish plans to facilitate the recruitment and advancement of disabled veterans. OPM provides information on veterans' federal service employment rights and privileges on the Internet: http://www.opm.gov/veterans/.

Veterans' Invitational Program (VIP)
OPM, in working with VA and the Department of Defense, established the Veterans' Invitational Program to encourage veterans to pursue a civilian career with the federal government. VIP officials conduct seminars nationwide that explain veterans' preference, appointing authorities, resume writing, interview skills and the federal application process. The program also provides educational tools and publications distributed to veteran service organizations, military transition offices and VA regional offices.

Miscellaneous Benefits

Loans for Farms and Homes
Loans and guarantees may be provided by the U.S. Department of Agriculture to buy, improve or operate farms. Loans and guarantees are available for housing in towns generally up to 20,000 in population. Applications from veterans have preference. For further information contact Farm Service Agency or Rural Development, U.S. Department of Agriculture, Washington, DC 20250, or apply at local Department of Agriculture offices, usually located in county seats.

Housing and Urban Development (HUD)
HUD homeless assistance grants are awarded to non-profit organizations, state and local governments, and public housing authorities to provide housing and services for the homeless, including those who are veterans or disabled veterans. Other HUD-funded activities

include homeownership assistance, micro enterprise development, job training and substance abuse counseling. HUD sponsors the Veteran Resource Center (HUDVET), which works with national veterans service organizations to serve as a general information center on all HUD sponsored housing and community development programs and services. To contact HUDVET, call 1-800-998-9999, TDD 800-483-2209, or e-mail hudvet@hud.gov. HUD also funds approved housing counseling agencies that provide free counseling services. To find a counselor, call toll-free 1-800-569-4287 or visit: www.hud.gov:80/offices/hsg/sfh/hcc/hcc_home.cfm.

Naturalization Preference

On July 3, 2002, the president issued Executive Order 13269 providing naturalization for aliens and non-citizen nationals serving on active duty status in the U.S. armed forces from Sept. 11, 2001, to a date not yet determined. In addition, if a person dies as a result of injury or disease incurred or aggravated by such service, their survivor(s) can apply for posthumous citizenship at any time within two years of the death of the alien or non-citizen national.

Veterans who served prior to Sept. 11, 2001, are eligible to file for naturalization based on their U.S. military service. An applicant who served three years in the U.S. military and is a lawful permanent resident is excused from any specific period of required residence, period of residence in any specific place, or physical presence within the United States if the application for naturalization is filed while the applicant is still serving in the military or within six months of honorable discharge. Applicants who file for naturalization more than six months after termination of three years of U.S. military service may count any periods of honorable service as residence and physical presence in the United States. For additional information, visit the U.S. Citizenship and Immigration Service Internet Web site: http://uscis.gov/graphics/services/natz/Special.htm.

Aliens and non-citizen nationals with honorable service in the U.S. armed forces during specified periods of hostilities may be naturalized without having to comply with the general requirements for naturalization. This is the only section of the Immigration and Nationality Act, as amended, which allows persons who have not been lawfully admitted for permanent residence to file an application for naturalization. Any person who has served honorably during qualifying time may file an application at any time in his or her life if, at the time of enlistment, reenlistment, extension of enlistment or induction, such person shall have been in the United States, the Canal Zone, American Samoa or Swain's Island, or, on or after Nov., 18, 1997, aboard a public vessel owned or operated by the United States for non-commercial service, whether or not lawful admittance to the United States for permanent residence has been granted.

Small Business Administration

The U.S. Small Business Administration's Office of Veterans Business Development provides a number of services to assist veterans who own or are considering starting small businesses. Among the services provided are loan guarantee programs, venture capital assistance, entrepreneurial development programs, government contracting assistance, and Military Reservist Economic Injury Disaster Loans. Information about SBA's full range of services can be found on the Internet: http://www.sba.gov/vets or by calling 202-205-6773. Veterans Business Development Officers at SBA District Offices can provide additional information. Call 1-800-U-ASK-SBA (1-800-827-5722) to locate the nearest SBA Office or for additional information.

Federal Tax Credits and Assistance

Federal law provides tax credits and special deductions that apply to many veterans or their families. The Earned Income Tax Credit may be available to low or moderate-income workers, depending on the amount of earned income and the number of qualifying children. Child Tax Credits may be available to taxpayers with children under age 17. Special deductions and credits can benefit disabled taxpayers or their families. Education credits and deductions for non-reimbursed educational expenses may be available to individuals when they or members of their family are pursuing post-secondary or job-related education. Free or low-cost income tax filing is available in many communities for low-income, elderly, disabled, and limited English proficient taxpayers. For additional information, visit http://www.irs.gov or call 1-800-829-1040.

Social Security

Monthly retirement, disability and survivor benefits under Social Security are payable to veterans and dependents if the veteran has earned enough work credits under the program. Upon the veteran's death, a one-time payment of $255 also may be made to the veteran's spouse or child. In addition, a veteran may qualify at age 65 for Medicare's hospital insurance and medical insurance. Medicare protection is available to people who have received Social Security disability benefits for 24 months, and to insured people and their dependents who need dialysis or kidney transplants, or who have amyotrophic lateral sclerosis (Lou Gehrig's disease).

Active duty or active duty for training in the U.S. uniformed services has counted toward Social Security since January 1957. Since Jan. 1, 1988, inactive duty for training as a member of reserve components of the armed forces also counts toward Social Security. Servicemembers and veterans receive an extra $300 credit for each quarter in which they received any basic pay for active duty or active duty for training after 1956 and before 1978. Veterans who served in the military from 1978 through 2001, receive a credit of $100 for each $300 of reported wages up to a maximum credit of $1,200. After 2001, additional earnings will no longer be credited. No additional Social Security taxes are withheld from pay for these extra credits. Also, noncontributory Social Security credits of $160 a month may be granted to veterans who served after Sept. 15, 1940, and before 1957, including attendance at service academies. For information, call 1-800-772-1213 or visit http://www.socialsecurity.gov.

Supplemental Security Income
Those age 65 or older and those who are blind or otherwise disabled may be eligible for monthly Supplemental Security Income (SSI) payments if they have little or no income or resources. States may supplement the federal payments to eligible persons and may disregard additional income. Although VA compensation and pension benefits are counted in determining income for SSI purposes, some other income is not counted. Also, not all resources count in determining eligibility. For example, a person's home and the land it is on do not count. Personal effects, household goods, automobiles and life insurance may not count, depending upon their value. Information and assistance in applying for these payments may be obtained at any Social Security office or by calling 1-800-772-1213.

Passports to Visit Overseas Cemeteries
"No-fee" passports are available for family members visiting graves or memorialization sites at World War I and World War II cemeteries overseas. Those eligible for such passports are limited to surviving spouses, parents, children, sisters, brothers and guardians of the deceased who are buried or commemorated in American military cemeteries on foreign soil. For additional information, write to the American Battle Monuments Commission, Courthouse Plaza II, Suite 500, 2300 Clarendon Blvd., Arlington, VA 22201, call 703-696-6897, or visit their Homepage: http://www.abmc.gov/.

Medals

Medals awarded while in active service are issued by the individual military services if requested by veterans or by the next of kin of deceased veterans. Requests for the issuance or replacement of military service medals, decorations, and awards should be directed to the specific branch of the military in which the veteran served. However, for Air Force (including Army Air Corps) and Army veterans, the National Personnel Records Center (NPRC) verifies the awards to which a veteran is entitled and forwards requests and verification to appropriate service department for issuance.

Requests for replacement medals should be submitted on Standard Form 180, "Request Pertaining To Military Records," which may be obtained at VA offices, from veterans organizations or downloaded from the Internet: http://www.vba.va.gov/pubs/otherforms.htm. The Military Personnel Records section of NPRC's Web site: http://www.archives.gov/facilities/mo/st_louis/military_personnel_records.html has forms, addresses and other information on requesting medals.

When requesting medals, type or clearly print the veteran's full name, include the veteran's branch of service, service number or Social Security Number and provide the veteran's exact or approximate dates of military service. The request must contain the signature of the veteran or the signature of the next of kin if the veteran is deceased. If available, include a copy of the discharge or separation document, WDAGO Form 53-55 or DD Form 214.

Review of Discharges

Each of the military services maintains a discharge review board with authority to change, correct or modify discharges or dismissals that are not issued by a sentence of a general courts-martial. The board has no authority to address medical discharges. The veteran or, if the veteran is deceased or incompetent, the surviving spouse, next of kin or legal representative may apply for a review of discharge by writing to the military department concerned, using DoD Form 293. This form may be obtained at a VA regional office, from veterans organizations or from the Internet: http://www.dtic.mil/whs/directives/infomgt/forms/formsprogram.htm. However, if the discharge was more than 15 years ago, a veteran must petition the appropriate service Board for Correction of Military Records using DoD Form 149, which is discussed in the "Correction of Military Records" section of this booklet. A discharge review is conducted by a review of an applicant's record and, if requested, by a hearing before the board.

Discharges awarded as a result of a continuous period of unauthorized absence in excess of 180 days make persons ineligible for VA benefits regardless of action taken by discharge review boards, unless VA determines there were compelling circumstances for the absence. Boards for the correction of military records also may consider such cases.

Veterans with disabilities incurred or aggravated during active military service may qualify for medical or related benefits regardless of separation and characterization of service. Veterans separated administratively under other than honorable conditions may request that their discharge be reviewed for possible recharacterization, provided they file their appeal within 15 years of the date of separation. Questions regarding the review of a discharge should be addressed to the appropriate discharge review board at the address listed on DoD Form 293.

Replacing Military Records

If discharge or separation papers are lost, veterans or the next of kin of deceased veterans may obtain duplicate copies by completing forms found on the Internet at: http://www.archives.gov/research_room/vetrecs/ and mailing or faxing them to the National Personnel Records Center. Alternatively, write the National Personnel Records Center, Military Personnel Records, 9700 Page Blvd., St. Louis, MO 63132-5100. Specify that a duplicate separation document or discharge is needed. The veteran's full name should be printed or typed so that it can be read clearly, but the request must also contain the signature of the veteran or the signature of the next of kin, if the veteran is deceased. Include branch of service, service number or Social Security number and exact or approximate dates and years of service. Use Standard Form 180, "Request Pertaining To Military Records." (See the "World Wide Web Links" section of this booklet for more information on obtaining this and other federal forms through the Internet, or contact your local VA regional office.) It is not necessary to request a duplicate copy of a veteran's discharge or separation papers solely for the purpose of filing a claim for VA benefits.

If complete information about the veteran's service is furnished on the application, VA will obtain verification of service from the National Personnel Records Center or the service department concerned.

Correction of Military Records

The secretary of a military department, acting through a board for correction of military records, has authority to change any military record when necessary to correct an error or remove an injustice. A correction board may consider applications for correction of a military record, including a review of a discharge issued by courts martial.

The veteran, survivor or legal representative generally must file a request for correction within three years after discovery of an alleged error or injustice. The board may excuse failure to file within the prescribed time, however, if it finds it would be in the interest of justice to do so. It is an applicant's responsibility to show why the filing of the application was delayed and why it would be in the interest of justice for the board to consider it despite the delay.

To justify a correction, it is necessary to show to the satisfaction of the board that the alleged entry or omission in the records was in error or unjust. Applications should include all available evidence, such as signed statements of witnesses or a brief of arguments supporting the correction. Application is made with DD Form 149, available at VA offices, from veterans organizations or on the Internet: http://www.dtic.mil/whs/directives/infomgt/forms/formsprogram.htm.

Armed Forces Retirement Home

Veterans are eligible to live in the Armed Forces Retirement Home in Gulfport, Miss., or Washington, D.C., if their active duty military service is at least 50 percent enlisted, warrant officer or limited duty officer if they are: 60 years of age or older and have completed 20 years or more of active duty service; unable to earn a livelihood due to a service-connected disability; unable to earn a livelihood due to a non-service connected disability and served in a war theater during a time of war declared by Congress or received hostile fire pay; female veterans who served prior to 1948.

Veterans are not eligible if they have been convicted of a felony or are not free from alcohol, drug or psychiatric problems. Married couples are welcome, but both must be eligible in their own right. At the time of admission, applicants must be capable of living independently.

The Armed Forces Retirement Home is an independent federal agency. For information, please call 1-800-332-3527 or 1-800-422-9988, or visit their Web site: http://www.afrh.gov/.

Commissary and Exchange Privileges

Unlimited exchange and commissary store privileges in the United States are available to honorably discharged veterans with a service-connected disability rated at 100 percent, unremarried surviving spouses of members or retired members of the armed forces, recipients of the Medal of Honor, and their dependents and orphans. Certification of total disability is done by VA. Reservists and their dependents also may be eligible. Privileges overseas are governed by international law and are available only if agreed upon by the foreign government concerned. Though these benefits are provided by DoD, VA does provide assistance in completing DD Form 1172, "Application for Uniformed Services Identification and Privilege Card." For detailed information, contact the nearest military installation.

Death Gratuity

Military services provide a death gratuity of $12,420 to a deceased servicemember's next of kin. The death gratuity is paid for death in active service or for retirees who died within 120 days of retirement as a result of service-connected injury or illness. Parents, brothers or sisters may be provided the gratuity, if designated as next of kin by the deceased. The gratuity is paid by the last military command of the deceased. If the beneficiary is not paid automatically, application may be made to the military service concerned.

Tables

2005 Disability Compensation

Disability	Monthly Rate ($)
10 percent	108
20 percent	210
30 percent	324
40 percent	466
50 percent	663
60 percent	839
70 percent	1,056
80 percent	1,227
90 percent	1,380
100 percent	2,299

Veterans with disability ratings between 30 percent and 100 percent are eligible for allowances for a spouse and for each minor child. The amount depends on the disability rating.

2005 Improved Disability Pension

Status	Maximum Annual Rate ($)
Veteran without dependent	10,162
Veteran with one dependent	13,309
Veteran permanently housebound, no dependents	12,419
Veteran permanently housebound, one dependent	15,566
Veteran needing regular aid and attendance, no dependents	16,955
Veteran needing regular aid and attendance, one dependent	20,099
Two veterans married to one another	13,309
Veterans of World War I and Mexican Border Period, addition to the applicable annual rate	2,305
Increase for each additional dependent child	1,734

Examples and more information can be found in the Compensation and Pension Benefits section of VA's Internet pages http://www.va.gov. Click on "Rate Tables."

2005 Vocational Rehabilitation Rates
(Paid monthly ($))

Type of training*	No dependent	One dep.	Two dep.	Each add. dep.
A				
Full-time	474.27	588.30	693.25	50.54
3/4-time	356.36	441.86	518.31	38.86
1/2-time	238.45	295.44	347.27	25.93
B				
Full-time	474.27	588.30	693.25	50.54
C				
Full-time	414.67	501.46	577.92	37.59
D				
Full-time	474.27	588.30	693.25	50.54
3/4-time	356.36	441.86	518.31	38.86
1/2-time	238.45	295.44	347.27	25.93
1/4-time	119.21	147.72	173.63	12.93

*Type of training

A. Institutional or independent living training, or unpaid work experience in a federal, state or local agency, or an agency of a federally recognized Indian tribe.

B. Unpaid on-the-job training in a federal, state or local agency, or an agency of a federally recognized Indian tribe; training in a home; vocational course in a rehabilitation facility or sheltered workshop; independent instructor; institutional non-farm cooperative.

C. Farm cooperative, apprenticeship, on-the-job training, or on-the-job non-farm cooperative. VA payment is based on the wage received.

D. Extended evaluation.

Spouses
2005 Dependency and Indemnity Compensation
(Veteran died prior to Jan. 1, 1993)

Pay Grade	Monthly Rate ($)
E-1-E-6	993
E-7	1,027
E-8	1,084
E-9	1,131
W-1	1,049
W-2	1,091
W-3	1,123
W-4	1,188
O-1	1,049
O-2	1,084
O-3	1,160
O-4	1,227
O-5	1,351
O-6	1,523
O-7	1,645
O-8	1,805
O-9	1,931
O-10	2,118

Spouses
2005 Dependency and Indemnity Compensation
(Veteran died on/after Jan. 1, 1993)

Allowances	Monthly Rate ($)
Basic Rate	$993
Additional:	
Each Dependent Child	247
Aid and Attendance	247
Housebound	118
Add $213 if veteran was totally disabled eight continuous years prior to death.	

2005 Improved Death Pension

Recipient	Maximum Annual Rate ($)
Surviving spouse With one dependent child	6,814 8,921
Surviving spouse permanently housebound With dependent child	8,328 10,432
Surviving spouse in need of regular aid and attendance With dependent child	 10,893 12,996
Allowance for each additional dependent child	1,734
Pension for each surviving child	1,734

Spina Bifida Benefits
(Effective Dec. 1, 2004)

	Level I	Level II	Level III
Monthly Rate ($)	244	844	1,440

Provided to children of Vietnam veterans born with spina bifida. The three levels represent degree of disability.

Benefits for Children of Women Vietnam Veterans Born with Certain Birth Defects
(Effective Dec. 1, 2004)

	Level I	Level II	Level III	Level IV
Monthly ($)	111	244	844	1,440

Provided to children of women Vietnam veterans who suffer from certain covered birth defects. The four levels represent degree of disability.

Important Phone Numbers

For information on:	Call:
VA Benefits	1-800-827-1000
Health Benefits	1-877-222-8387
Education Benefits	1-888-442-4551
Life Insurance	1-800-669-8477
Debt Management	1-800-827-0648
Mammography Hotline	1-888-492-7844
Telecommunication Device for the Deaf (TDD)	1-800-829-4833
CHAMPVA	1-800-733-8387
Headstones and Markers	1-800-697-6947
Special Health Issues: Gulf War, Agent Orange, Project 112/Shad	1-800-749-8387
Health Eligibility Center 2957 Clairmont Rd. #200 Atlanta, GA 30329	404-235-1257 or 1-800-929-8387

This VA Federal Benefits booklet and other information is available on VA's World Wide Web Home Page at:

http://www.va.gov/

Veterans Benefits on the Internet

VA Home page... www.va.gov
VA consumer affairs........................ www.va.gov/customer/conaff.asp

VA Benefits and Health Care Information:
Compensation & Pension............................... www.vba.va.gov/bln/21/
VA benefits application........................ vabenefits.vba.va.gov/vonapp
Health benefits and services........................ www.va.gov/vbs/health/
Burial and memorial benefits................................ www.cem.va.gov/
Education benefits.. www.gibill.va.gov/
VA home loan guaranties.......................... www.homeloans.va.gov/
Board of Veterans' Appeals............................ www.va.gov/vbs/bva
Benefits outside the U.S.................. www.vba.va.gov/bln/21/foreign/
TRICARE.. www.tricare.osd.mil/
CHAMPVA.. www.va.gov/hac/

Forms:
VA forms.. www.va.gov/forms/
Other government forms.......... www.vba.va.gov/pubs/otherforms.htm

Employment Assistance:
Veterans' preference........ www.opm.gov/veterans/html/vetguide.asp
Federal government job openings................. www.usajobs.opm.gov/
Dept. of Labor .... www.dol.gov/vets/welcome.html

Business Assistance:
Small Business Administration......................... www.sba.gov/VETS/
Small and Disadvantaged Businesses.............. www.va.gov/OSDBU/

Other Useful Sites:
Arlington National Cemetery.................... www.arlingtoncemetery.org/
Department of Defense.. www.defenselink.mil/
Military funeral honors................. www.militaryfuneralhonors.osd.mil/
Military records................. www.archives.gov/research_room/vetrecs/

La Versión en Español de Este Folleto:
www.va.gov/opa/feature/

VA Facilities

Note: Patients should call the telephone numbers listed to obtain clinic hours of operation and services. The following symbols indicate additional programs are available at medical centers:

* for nursing-home care units
# for domiciliaries

Please send address and telephone number corrections to:

Federal Benefits for Veterans and Dependents (80D)
810 Vermont Ave. NW
Washington, DC 20420

ALABAMA
Medical Centers:
Central AL Veterans HC System (1-800-214-8387):
   Montgomery 36109 (215 Perry Hill Rd., 334-272-4670)
   #*Tuskegee 36083 (2400 Hospital Rd., 334-727-0550)
Birmingham 35233 (700 S. 19th St., 205-933-8101)
*Tuscaloosa 35404 (3701 Loop Rd. East, 205-554-2000)
Clinics:
Anniston/Oxford 36203 (96 Ali Way, Creekside South, 256-832-4141)
Decatur/Madison 35758 (8075 Madison Blvd., Suite 101, 256-772-6220)
Dothan 36301 (2020 Alexander Dr., 334-679-4166)
Dothan MHC 36301 (3753 Ross Clark Cir., Suite 4, 334-678-1903)
Florence Shoals Area 35660 (422 DD Cox Blvd., 256-381-9055)
Gadsden 35906 (206 Rescia Ave., 256-413-7154)
Huntsville 35801 (301 Governor's Dr., S.W., 256-535-3100)
Jasper 35501 (3400 Hwy 78 East, Medical Towers Suite 215, 205-221-7384)
Mobile 36604 (1504 Springhill Ave., 251-219-3900)
Regional Office:
Montgomery 36109 (345 Perry Hill Rd., statewide, 1-800-827-1000)
Vet Centers:
Birmingham 35233 (1500 5th Ave. S., 205-731-0550)
Mobile 36606 (2577 Government Blvd., 251-478-5906)

National Cemeteries:
Fort Mitchell NC 36856 (553 Hwy. 165, Seale, 334-855-4731)
Mobile NC 36604 (1202 Virginia St., 850-453-4108/4846)

ALASKA
Medical Center:
Alaska VA Healthcare System and Regional Office:
Anchorage 99508-2989 (2925 DeBarr Rd, 907-257-4700)
#Homeless Veterans: Anchorage 99503 (3001 C St., 1-800-764-2995)
Clinics:
Kenai 99611 (805 Frontage Rd., Suite 130, 1-877-797-8924)
Fairbanks 99703 (Ft. Wainwright, Bassett Army Hospital, Gaffney Bldg. 4065, Rm. 169/176, 907-353-6370)
Regional Office:
Anchorage 99508-2989 (2925 De Barr Rd., statewide, 1-800-827-1000)
Benefits Office:
Juneau 99802 (P.O. Box 20069, 907-586-7472)
Vet Centers:
Anchorage 99508 (4201 Tudor Centre Dr., Suite 115, 907-563-6966)
Fairbanks 99701 (540 4th Ave., Suite 100, 907-456-4238)
Kenai 99669 (43335 Kalifornsky Beach Rd., Bldg. F, Suite 4, 907-260-7640)
Wasilla 99654 (851 E. West Point Dr., Suite 111, 907-376-4318)
National Cemeteries:
Fort Richardson NC 99505-5498 (Bldg. 997, Davis Highway, 907-384-7075)
Sitka NC 99835 (803 Sawmill Creek Rd., 907-384-7075)

AMERICAN SAMOA
Benefits Office:
Pago Pago 96799 (PO Box 1005, 684-633-5071)

ARIZONA
Medical Centers:
*Phoenix 85012 (650 East Indian School Rd., 602-277-555, ext. 6508)
*#Prescott 86313 (500 Highway 89 North, 928-445-4860)
*Tucson 85723 (3601 S. 6th Ave., 520-792-1450)
Clinics:
Anthem 85086 (3618 W. Anthem Way, Bldg., 120D, 928-445-4860 ext. 7200)
Bellemont 86015 (Camp Navajo Army Depot, P.O. Box 16196, 928-445-4860 ext. 7820 or 928-226-1056)
Buckeye 85326 (1209 N. Miller Rd., 623-386-5785)
Cottonwood 86326 (203 Candy Lane, Suite 5B, 928-649-1532)
Casa Grande 85222 (Plaza del Sol, 900 E. Florence Blvd., Suites H&I, 520-836-2536 or 1-800-470-8262)
Green Valley 85615 (380 W. Vista Hermosa, Suite 140, 1-800-470-8262)
Kingman 86401 (1726 Beverly Ave., 928-445-4860 ext. 6830)
Lake Havasu City 86403 (2035 Mesquite Ave., Southeast, 928-445-4860 ext. 7300 or 928-680-0090)
Mesa 85212 (6950 E. Williams Field Rd., 602-222-6568)

Payson 85541 (1106 N. Beeline Hwy., 928-472-3148)
Safford 85546 (Bureau of Land Mgmt., 711 S. 14th Ave., 520-629-4900)
Show Low 85901(2450 Show Low Lake Rd., Suite 1 & 3, 928-532-1069)
Sierra Vista 85613 (Ft. Huachuca, Bliss Army Health Ctr., Bldg. 45001,
    520-629-4900 or 1-800-470-8262)
Sun City 85351 (10147W Grand Ave., Suite C, 602-222-2630, ext. 3732)
Yuma 85365 (Bureau of Land Mgmt., 2555 E. Gila Ridge Rd., 520-629-4900)
Regional Office:
Phoenix 85012 (3333 N. Central Ave.; statewide, 1-800-827-1000)
Vet Centers:
Phoenix 85012 (77 E. Weldon Ave., Suite 100, 602-640-2981)
Prescott 86303 (161 S. Granite St., Suite B, 928-778-3469)
Tucson 85719 (3055 N. 1st Ave., 520-882-0333)
National Cemeteries:
Nat. Cem. of AZ 85024 (23029 N. Cave Creek Rd., Phoenix, 480-513-3600)
Prescott NC 86301 (500 Highway 89 N., 480-513-3600)

ARKANSAS
Medical Centers:
Fayetteville 72703 (1100 N. College Ave., 479-443-4301)
Central Arkansas Veterans Healthcare System
    #*North Little Rock 72114 (2200 Fort Roots Dr., 501-257-1000)
    Little Rock 72205 (4300 W. 7th St., 501-257-1000)
Clinics:
El Dorado 71730 (460 West Oak, 870-862-2489)
Ft. Smith 72917 (Sparks Medical Plaza, 1500 Dodson Ave., 479 709-6850)
Harrison 72601 (Main Street Clinic, 707 N. Main St., 870 741-3592)
Hot Springs 71913 (1661 Airport Rd., 501-760-1513)
Jonesboro 72401 (223 East Jackson, 901-523-8990)
Mountain Home 72653 (405 Buttercup Dr., 870-425-3030)
Paragould 72450 (1101 West Morgan, Suite 8, 870-236-9756)
Texarkana 71854 (910 Realtor Ave., 870-216-2242)
Regional Office:
North Little Rock 72114 (2200 Fort Roots Dr., Bldg. 65, 1-800-827-1000)
Vet Center:
North Little Rock 72114 (201 W. Broadway, Suite A, 501-324-6395)
National Cemeteries:
Fayetteville NC 72701 (700 Government Ave., 501-444-5051)
Fort Smith NC 72901 (522 Garland Ave., 501-783-5345)
Little Rock NC 72206 (2523 Confederate Blvd., 501-324-6401)

CALIFORNIA
Medical Centers:
*Fresno 93703 (2615 E. Clinton Ave., 559-225-6100)
Greater Los Angeles HC System:
    #*West Los Angeles 90073 (11301 Wilshire Blvd., 310-478-3711)
Loma Linda 92357 (11201 Benton St., 909-825-7084 or 1-800-741-8387)
Long Beach 90822 (5901 E. 7th St., 562-826-8000)

Northern Calif. HC System:
*Martinez 94553 (150 Muir Rd., 925-372-2000)
Sacramento 95655 (10535 Hospital Way, 916-843-7000)
Palo Alto HC System:
*Livermore 94550 (4951 Arroyo Rd., 925-373-4700)
#Menlo Park 94025 (795 Willow Rd., 650-493-5000)
#*Palo Alto 94304 (3801 Miranda Ave., 650-493-5000)
San Diego HC System:
*San Diego 92161 (3350 La Jolla Village Dr., 858-552-8585)
*San Francisco 94121 (4150 Clement St., 415-221-4810)
Clinics:
Anaheim 92801 (1801 W. Romneya Drive, Suite 303, 714-780-5400)
Antelope Valley/Lancaster 93536 (547 W. Lancaster Blvd., 661-729-8655)
Atwater 95301 (3605 Hospital Road, Suite D, 209-381-0105)
Auburn 95603 (3123 Professional Drive, Suite 250, 1-888-227-5404)
Bakersfield 93301 (1801 Westwind Dr., 661-632-1800)
Brawley/Imperial Valley 92227 (528 G. St., 760-344-1881)
Capitola 95010 (co-located at Santa Cruz Co. Vet Center, 1350 N. 41st St., Suite 102, 831-464-5519)
Chico 95926 (280 Cohasset Rd., Suite 101, 530-879-5000)
Chula Vista 91910 (835 Third Avenue, 619-409-1600)
Corona 92879 (800 Magnolia Ave, Suite 101, 951-817-8820)
Culver City 90230 (3831 Hughes Avenue, Ste. 100, 310-202-8223)
East Los Angeles 90040 (5400 E. Olympic Blvd., #150, City of Commerce, 323-725-7557)
Escondido 92025 (815 East Pennsylvania Ave., 760-466-7020)
Eureka 95501 (714 F St., 707-442-5335)
Fairfield 94535 (103 Bodin Circle, Building 778, Travis AFB, 707-437-1800)
Gardena 90247 (1251 Redondo Beach Blvd., 3rd Fl., 310-851-4705)
Long Beach 90806 (2001 River Ave., Bldg. 28, 562-388-8000)
Los Angeles 90012 (351 E. Temple St., 213-253-5000)
Mare Island 94592 (Bldg. 201, Walnut Ave., 707-562-8200)
*Martinez 94553 (150 Muir Rd., 925-372-2000)
McClellan AFB 95652 (5342 Dudley Blvd., 916-561-7400)
Mission Valley 92108 (8810 Rio San Diego Drive, 619-400-5000)
Modesto 95350 (1524 McHenry, Suite 315, 209-557-6200)
Monterey 93955 (located at Fort Ord, 3401 Engineer Lane, Seaside, 831-883-3800)
Oakland 94612 (2221 Martin Luther King Jr. Way, 510-267-7820)
Oakland MHC 94607 (Army Base, 2505 W. 14th St., 510-587-3400)
Oxnard 93030 (250 W. Citrus Grove Ave., #150, 805-983-6384)
Palm Desert 92211 (41865 Boardwalk, Suite 103, 760-341-5570)
Pasadena 91107 (1350 N. Altadena Dr., 626-296-9514)
Redding 96002 (351 Hartnell Ave., 530-226-7555)
Sacramento 95652-1074 (5342 Dudley Blvd. McClellan Park AFB, 916-561-7400)
San Francisco 94103 (205 13th St., Suite 2150, 415-551-7300)
San Jose 95119 (80 Great Oaks Blvd., 408-363-3000)

San Luis Obispo 93401 (1288 Morro St., #200, 805-543-1233)
Santa Ana 92704 (2740 S. Bristol St., Ste. 101, 714-825-3500)
Santa Fe Springs 90670 (10210 Orr and Day Rd., 562-864-5565)
Santa Barbara 93110 (4440 Calle Real, 805-683-1491)
Santa Rosa 95404 (3315 Chanate Rd., 707-570-3855)
*Sepulveda 91343 (16111 Plummer St., 818-891-7711)
Sonora 95370 (19747 Greenley Rd., 209-588-2600)
Stockton 95231 (co-located with San Joaquin General Hospital, 500 W. Hospital Rd., 209-946-3400)
Sun City 92586 (28125 Bradley Rd., #130, 909-672-1931)
Tulare 93274 (1050 N. Cherry St., 559-684-8703)
Ukiah 95482 (630 Kings Ct., 707-468-7700)
Upland 91786 (1238 E. Arrow Hwy., #100, 909-946-5348)
Victorville 92392 (12138 Industrial Blvd., Suite 120, 800-741-8387)
Vista 92083 (1840 West Dr., 760-643-2000)

Regional Offices:
Los Angeles 90024 (Fed. Bldg., 11000 Wilshire Blvd., serving counties of Inyo, Kern, Los Angeles, Orange, San Bernardino, San Luis Obispo, Santa Barbara and Ventura; statewide, 1-800-827-1000)
Oakland 94612 (1301 Clay St., Rm. 1300 North; statewide, 1-800-827-1000)
Counties of Alpine, Lassen, Modoc and Mono served by Reno, Nev., VARO

Benefits Offices:
San Diego 92108 (8810 Rio San Diego Dr., serving Imperial, Riverside and San Diego; statewide, 1-800-827-1000)
Sacramento 95827 (10365 Old Placerville Rd., 916-364-6500)

Vet Centers:
Anaheim 92805 (859 S. Harbor Blvd., 714-776-0161)
Chico 95926 (280 Cohasset Rd., Suite 100, 530-899-8549)
Concord 94520 (1899 Clayton Rd., Suite 140, 925-680-4526)
Corona 92879 (800 Magnolia Ave., #140, 951-734-0525)
East Los Angeles 90022 (5400 E. Olympic Blvd., #140, 323-728-9966)
Eureka 95501 (2830 G St., Suite A, 707-444-8271)
Fresno 93726 (3636 N. 1st St., Suite 112, 559-487-5660)
Gardena 90247 (1045 W. Redondo Beach Blvd., #150, 310-767-1221)
West Los Angeles 90230 (5730 Uplander Way, Suite 100, Culver City, 310-641-0326)
Marina 93933 (455 Reservation Rd., Suite E, 408-384-1660)
Oakland 94612 (1504 Franklin St., #200, 510-763-3904)
Redwood City 94062 (2946 Broadway St., 650-299-0672)
Rohnert Park 94928 (6225 State Farm Dr., Suite 101, 707-586-3295)
Sacramento 95825 (1111 Howe Ave., Suite 390, 916-566-7430)
San Bernardino 92408 (155 W. Hospitality Lane, Suite 140, 619-294-2040)
San Diego 92103 (2900 6th Ave., 619-294-2040)
San Francisco 94102 (505 Polk St., 415-441-5051)
San Jose 95112 (278 N. 2nd St., 408-993-0729)
Sepulveda 91343 (9737 Haskell Ave., 818-892-9227)
Ventura 93001 (790 E. Santa Clara, 805-585-1860)
Vista 92083 (1830 West Dr., Suite 103, 760-643-2070)

National Cemeteries:
Fort Rosecrans NC 92106 (P.O. Box 6237, Point Loma, San Diego, 619-553-2084)
Golden Gate NC 94066 (1300 Sneath Ln., San Bruno (San Francisco call 650-761-1646; San Mateo call 650-589-7737))
Los Angeles NC 90049 (950 South Sepulveda Blvd., 310-268-4494)
Riverside NC 92518 (22495 Van Buren Blvd., 951-653-8417)
San Francisco NC 94129 (P.O. Box 29012, Presidio, 650-589-7737)
San Joaquin Valley NC 95322 (32053 W. McCabe Rd., Gustine, 209-854-1040)

COLORADO
Medical Centers:
*Grand Junction 81501 (2121 North Ave., 970-242-0731)
VA Eastern Colorado HC System
 Denver 80220 (1055 Clermont St., 303-399-8020 or 1-888-336-8262)
Clinics:
Alamosa 81101 (622 Del Sol Dr., 719-587-6800 or toll free 1-866-659-0930)
Aurora 80045 (13001 East 17th Place, Bldg. 500, 2nd floor, 303-724-0190)
Colorado Springs 80905 (25 N. Spruce St., 719-327-5660)
Durango 81301 (3575 N. Main Ave., 970-247-2214)
Fort Collins 80524 (1100 Poudre River Dr., 970-224-1550)
Greeley 80631 (2020 16th St., 970-313-0027)
LaJunta 81050 (1100 Carson Ave., Suite 104, 719-383-5195)
Lakewood 80228 (155 Van Gordon St., Suite 395, 303-914-2680)
Lamar 81052 (201 Kendall Dr., 719-336-5972)
Montrose 81401 (4 Hillcrest Plaza Way, 970-249-7791)
Pueblo, CO 81003 (4112 Outlook Blvd., 719-553-1000)
Regional Office:
Denver 80225 (Box 25126; statewide, 1-800-827-1000)
Vet Centers:
Boulder 80302 (2336 Canyon Blvd., Suite 130, 303-440-7306)
Colorado Springs 80903 (416 E. Colorado Ave., 719-471-9992)
Denver 80230 (7465 E. First Ave., Ste. B, 303-326-0645)
National Cemeteries:
Fort Logan NC 80235 (3698 S. Sheridan Blvd., Denver, 303-761-0117)
Fort Lyon NC 81038 (303-761-0117)

CONNECTICUT
Medical Centers:
Conn. HC System:
 *West Haven Division 06516 (950 Campbell Ave., 203-932-5711)
 Newington Division 06111 (555 Willard Ave., 860-666-6951)
Clinics:
Danbury 06810 (7 Germantown Rd., 203-798-8422)
Stamford 06924 (90 Morgan St., 203-325-0649)
New London 06320 (15 Mohegan Ave., 860-437-3611)
Waterbury 06706 (133 Scovill St., Suite 203, 203-465-5292)

Windham 06226 (96 Mansfield St., 860-450-7583)
Winsted 06098 (115 Spencer St., 860-738-6985)
Regional Office:
Hartford 06111-2693 (555 Willard Ave., Bldg 2E – RM 5137, Newington, statewide, 1-800-827-1000)
Vet Centers:
Wethersfield 06109 (30 Jordan Lane, 860-563-2320)
Norwich 06360 (2 Cliff St., 860-887-1755)
West Haven 06516 (141 Captain Thomas Blvd., 203-932-9899)

DELAWARE
Medical Center:
*Wilmington 19805 (1601 Kirkwood Hwy., 1-800-461-8262)
Clinic:
Millsboro 19966 (214 W. DuPont Hwy., 302-934-0195)
Regional Office:
Wilmington 19805 (1601 Kirkwood Hwy., local, 302-994-2511)
Vet Center:
Wilmington 19805 (1601 Kirkwood Hwy., Bldg. 3, 302-994-1660)

DISTRICT OF COLUMBIA
Medical Center:
*Washington, D.C. 20422 (50 Irving St., N.W., 202-745-8000)
Clinic:
Southeast 20032 (820 Chesapeake St., S.E., 202-745-8685)
Regional Office:
Washington, D.C. 20421 (1722 I St., N.W., local, 1-800-827-1000)
Vet Center:
Washington, D.C. 20011 (1250 Taylor St., N.W., 202-726-5212)

FLORIDA
Medical Centers:
#*Bay Pines 33744 (10000 Bay Pines Blvd., 727-398-6661)
N. Florida/S. Georgia Veterans Health System:
  *Gainesville 32608 (1601 Southwest Archer Rd., 352-376-1611)
  *Lake City 32025 (619 S. Marion Ave., 386-755-3016)
*Miami 33125 (1201 N.W. 16th St., 305-575-7000)
*Tampa 33612 (13000 Bruce B. Downs Blvd., 813-972-2000)
*West Palm Beach 33410 (7305 N. Military Trail, 561-422-8262)
Clinics:
Boca Raton 33433 (900 Glades Rd., 561-416-8995)
Brooksville 34613 (14540 Cortez Blvd., Suite 202, 352-597-8287)
Coral Springs 33065 (9900 W. Sample Rd., Suite 100, 954-575-4940)
Daytona Beach 32114 (551 National Health Care Dr., 386-274-4600)
Deerfield Beach 33442 (2100 SW 10th St., 954-570-5572)
Delray Beach 33445 (4800 Linton Blvd, 561-495-1973)
Dunedin 34698 (1721 Main St., 727-734-5276)
Ellenton 34222 (4333 U.S. Hwy 301 North, 941-721-0649)

Fort Myers 33916 (3033 Winkler Extension, 239-939-3939)
Ft. Pierce 34950 (727 North US 1, 561-595-5150)
Hollywood 33021 (3702 Washington St., Pavilion, Suite 201, 954-986-1811)
Homestead 33030 (950 Krome Ave., Suite 401, 305-248-0874)
Inverness 34453 (401 North Central Ave., 352 637-3500)
Jacksonville 32206 (1833 Boulevard St., 904-232-3033)
Key Largo 33037 (105662 Overseas Highway, 305-451-0164)
Key West 33040 (1300 Douglas Cir., 305-293-4609)
Kissimmee 34741 (201 Hilda St., Kissimmee, 407-518-5004)
Lakeland 33803 (3240 S. Florida Ave., Lakeland, 863-701-2470)
Leesburg 34788 (711 West Main Blvd., 352-728-4462)
Naples 34101 (2685 Horseshoe Dr., S, Suite 101, 239-659-9188)
New Port Richey 34642 (9912 Little Rd., 727-869-4100)
Oakland Park 33334 (5599 N. Dixie Highway, 954-771-2101)
Ocala 34470 (1515 E. Silver Springs Blvd., 352-369-3320)
Okeechobee 34972 (1201 N. Parrott Ave., 863 824-3232)
Orlando 32803 (5201 Raymond St., 407-629-1599)
Panama City 32407 (6703 West Hwy 98, Bldg. 387, 850-636-7000)
Pembroke Pines/Hollywood 33024 (7369 Sheridan St., Suite 102, 954-894-1668)
Pensacola South 32503 (312 Kenmore Rd., 850-476-1100)
Pensacola North 32506 (7895-C Pensacola Blvd., 850-476-1100)
Port Charlotte 33952 (Opening June 2005 at 4161 Tamiami Trail, Ste. 401)
Sanford 32771 (1403 Medical Plaza Dr., Suite 109, 407-323-5999)
Sarasota 34233 (5682 Bee Ridge Rd., Suite 100, 941-371-3349)
Sebring 33870 (3760 US Hwy. 27 South, 863-471-6227)
St. Petersburg 33711 (3420 8th Avenue South, 727-322-1304)
St. Augustine 32086 (1955 US 1 South, Suite 200, 904 829-0814)
Stuart 34997 (3501 SE Willoughby Blvd., 561-288-0304)
Tallahassee 32308 (1607 St. James Ct., 850-878-0191)
Vero Beach 32960 (1485 37th St., Suite 102, 561-299-4623)
Viera 32940 (2900 Veterans Way, 321-637-3788)
Zephyrhills 33541 (37814 Medical Arts Ct., 813-780-2550)
Regional Office:
St. Petersburg 33708 (P.O. Box 1437; statewide, 1-800-827-1000)
Benefits Offices: Call *1-800-827-1000*
Fort Lauderdale 33301 (VR&E, 299 East Broward Blvd., Room 324)
Jacksonville 32256 (VR&E, 7825 Baymeadows Way, Suite 120-B)
Orlando 32801 (1000 Legion Place, VR&E Suite 1500, C&P Suite 1550)
Pensacola 32503-7492 (C&P, 312 Kenmore Rd., Rm. 1G250)
West Palm Beach 33410 (C&P, 7305 North Military Trail, Suite 1A-167)
Vet Centers:
Ft. Lauderdale 33304 (713 N.E. 3rd Ave., 954-356-7926)
Jacksonville 32202 (300 East State St., 904-232-3621)
Miami 33129 (2700 S.W. 3rd Ave., Suite1A, 305-859-8387)
Orlando 32822 (5575 S. Semoran Blvd., Suite 36, 407-857-2800)
Palm Beach 33461 (2311 10th Ave., North #13, 561-585-0441)
Pensacola 32501 (4501 Twin Oaks Dr., 850-456-5886)

Sarasota 34231 (4801 Swift Rd., 941-927-8285)
St. Petersburg 33713 (2880 1st Ave., N., 727-893-3791)
Tallahassee 32303 (548 Bradford Rd., 850-942-8810)
Tampa 33604 (8900 N. Armenia Ave., #312, 813-228-2621)
National Cemeteries:
Barrancas NC 32508-1099 (80 Hovey Rd., Naval Air Station, Pensacola, 850-453-4108/4846)
Bay Pines NC 33504-0477 (10000 Bay Pines Blvd., North Bay Pines, 727-398-9426)
Florida NC 33513 (6502 SW 102nd Ave., Bushnell, 352-793-7740)
St. Augustine NC 32084 (104 Marine St., 352-793-7740)

GEORGIA
Medical Centers:
*Augusta 30904 (1 Freedom Way, 706-823-1738)
*Decatur 30033 (1670 Clairmont Rd., 404-321-6111)
#*Dublin 31021 (1826 Veterans Blvd., 478-272-1210)
Clinics:
Albany 31701 (417 4th Ave., 229-446-9000 or 1-877-216-4495)
Atlanta 30309 (77 Peachtree Place, 404-321-6111, ext. 2600)
Columbus 31906 (1310 13th Ave., 706-257-7200)
Lawrenceville 30043 (1970 Riverside Pkwy., 404-417-1750)
Macon 31220 (5398 Thomaston Rd., Suite B, 1-800-552-7483)
Oakwood 30566 (3931 Mundy Mill Rd., Suite C, 404-728-8210)
Savannah 31406 (325 W. Montgomery Crossroad, 912-920-0214)
Smyrna 30082 (562 Concord Rd., S.E., 404-417-1760)
Valdosta 31602 (2841 North Patterson, 229-293-0132)
Regional Office:
Decatur 30033 (1700 Clairmont Rd., statewide, 1-800-827-1000)
Vet Centers:
Atlanta 30324 (1440 Dutch Valley Place, Suite G, 404-347-7264)
Savannah 31406 (8110A White Bluff Rd., 912-652-4097)
National Cemetery:
Marietta NC 30060 (500 Washington Ave., 866-236-8159)

GUAM
Clinic:
Agana Heights 96919 (U.S. Naval Hospital, Bldg-1, E-200, Box 7608, 671-344-9200)
Benefits Office/Vet Center:
Hagatna 96910 (222 Chalan Santo Papa, Reflection Center, 671-472-7161)

HAWAII
Medical Center:
Honolulu 96819-1522 (459 Patterson Rd., 808-433-0600)
Clinics:
Hilo 96720 (1285 Wainuenue Ave., Suite 211, 808-935-3781)
Kauai; Lihue 96766 (3-3367 Kuhio Hwy, Suite 200, 808-246-0497)

Kona; Kailua-Kona 96740 (75-5995 Kuakini Hwy, Suite 413, 808-329-0774)
Maui; Kahului 96732 (203 Ho'ohana St., Suite 303, 808-871-2454)
Regional Office:
Honolulu 96819-1522 (459 Patterson Rd., E Wing, toll-free from Hawaii, 1-800-827-1000; toll-free from Guam, 1-800-827-2166; toll-free from American Samoa, 1-877-285-1128; toll-free from Saipan, Rota and Tinian, 1-888-253-2750)
Benefits Offices:
Hilo 96720 (VR&E, 891 Ululani St., 808-961-3413)
Kahului 96732 (VR&E, 203 Ho'ohana St., 808-873-9426)
Vet Centers:
Hilo 96720 (120 Keawe St., Suite 201, 808-969-3833)
Honolulu 96814 (1680 Kapiolani Blvd., Suite F.3, 808-973-8387)
Kailua-Kona 96740 (Pottery Terrace, Fern Bldg., 75-5995 Kuakini Hwy., 415, 808-329-0574)
Lihue 96766 (3-3367 Kuhio Hwy., Suite 101, 808-246-1163)
Wailuku 96793 (35 Lunalilo, Suite 101, 808-242-8557)
National Cemetery:
Nat. Mem. Cem. of the Pacific 96813-1729 (2177 Puowaina Dr., Honolulu, 808-532-3720)

IDAHO
Medical Center:
*Boise 83702 (500 West Fort St., 208-422-1000)
Clinics:
Pocatello 83201 (444 Hospital Way, Suite 801, 208-232-6214)
Twin Falls 83301 (260 2nd Ave, E., 208-732-0947)
Regional Office:
Boise 83702 (805 W. Franklin St.; statewide, 1-800-827-1000)
Vet Centers:
Boise 83705 (5440 Franklin Rd., Suite 100, 208-342-3612)
Pocatello 83201 (1800 Garrett Way, 208-232-0316)

ILLINOIS
Medical Centers:
Chicago 60612 (820 S. Damen Ave., 312-569-8387)
* Danville 61832 (900 E. Main St., 217-554-3000 or 800-320-8387)
*Hines 60141 (Roosevelt Rd. & 5th Ave., 708-202-8387)
*Marion 62959 (2401 W. Main St., 618-997-5311)
#*North Chicago 60064 (3001 Green Bay Rd., 847-688-1900)
Clinics:
Aurora 60506 (1700 N. Landmark Rd., 630-859-2504)
Belleville 62223 (6500 W. Main St., 618-398-2100)
Chicago--Lakeside 60611 (333 E. Huron 312-569-8387)
Chicago 60643 (2038 W. 95th St., 773-239-7134)
Chicago Heights 60411 (30 E. 15th St. Suite 207, 708-756-5454)
Decatur 62526 (3035 E. Mound Rd., 217-875-2670 or 800-320-8387)
Effingham 62401 (Lincolnland Bldg., 1901 S. 4th St., 217-347-7600)

Elgin 60123 (1231 N. Larkin Blvd., 847-742-5920)
Evanston 60202 (107 -109 Clyde St., 847-869-6315)
Freeport 61032 (1301 Kiwanis Dr., 608-280-7038)
Galesburg 61401 (695 N. Kellogg St, 309-343-0311)
Joliet 60435 (2000 Glenwood Ave., 815-744-0492)
LaSalle 61301 (2970 Chartres St., 815-223-9678)
Manteno 60950 (One Veterans Drive, 815-468-1027)
McHenry 60050 (620 S. Route 31, 815-759-2306)
Mt. Vernon 62864, (1 Doctors Park Rd, 618-246-2910 or 2911)
Oak Lawn 60453 (4700 W. 95th St., Suite 104, 708-499-3675)
Oak Park 60302 (149 S. Oak Park Ave., 708-386-3008)
Peoria 61605 (411 Martin Luther King Jr. Dr., 800-320-8387)
Quincy 62301 (1707 North 12th St., 217-224-3366)
Rockford 61108 (4940 East State St., 815-227-0081)
Springfield 62702 (700 N. 7th St., 217-522-9730 or 800-320-8387)
Regional Office:
Chicago 60612 (2122 W. Taylor St., P.O. Box 8136; 1-800-827-1000)
Vet Centers:
Chicago 60643 (2038 W. 95th St., Suite 200, 773-881-9900)
Chicago Heights 60411 (1600 S. Halsted St., 708-754-0340)
East St. Louis 62203 (1269 N. 89th St., Suite 1, 618-397-6602)
Evanston 60202 (565 Howard St., 847-332-1019)
Moline 61265 (1529 46th Ave., 6, 309-762-6954)
Oak Park 60302 (155 S. Oak Park Blvd., 708-383-3225)
Peoria 61603 (3310 N. Prospect Rd., 309-671-7300)
Springfield 62702 (624 S. 4th St., 217-492-4955)
National Cemeteries:
Abraham Lincoln NC 60421 (27034 South Diagonal Rd., Elwood, 815-423-9958)
Alton NC 62003 (600 Pearl St., 314-260-8720)
Camp Butler NC 62707 (5063 Camp Butler Rd., Springfield, 217-492-4070)
Danville NC 61832 (1900 East Main St., 217-554-4550)
Mound City NC 62963 (Junction Hwy., 37 & 51, 314-260-8720)
Quincy NC 62301 (36th and Maine St., 309-782-2094)
Rock Island NC 61299-7090 (Rock Island Arsenal, Bldg. 118, 309-782-2094)

INDIANA
Medical Centers:
Indianapolis 46202 (1481 W. 10th St., 317-554-0000)
Northern Indiana HC System:
 *Fort Wayne 46805 (2121 Lake Ave., 260-426-5431)
 *Marion 46953 (1700 E. 38th St., 765-674-3321)
Clinics:
Bloomington 47403 (455 S. Landmark Ave., 812-335-2400)
Crown Point 46307 (9330 S. Broadway, 219-662-5000)
Evansville 47713 (500 E. Walnut, 812-465-6202)
Lawrenceburg 47025 (710 W. Eads Pkwy, 812-539-2313)
Muncie/Anderson 47304 (3500 W. Purdue Ave., 765-284-6822)

New Albany 47150 (811 Northgate Boulevard, 502-287-4100)
Richmond 47374 (4351 South A St., 765-973-6915)
South Bend 46614 (5735 W. Ironwood Dr., 574-229-4847)
Terre Haute 47802 (110 W. Honeycreek Pkwy, 812-232-2890)
West Lafayette 47906 (3851 N. River Rd., 1-800-320-8387)
Regional Office:
Indianapolis 46204 (575 N. Pennsylvania St., statewide 1-800-827-1000)
Vet Centers:
Evansville 47711 (311 N. Weinbach Ave., 812-473-5993 or 473-6084)
Fort Wayne 46802 (528 West Berry St., 260-460-1456)
Merrillville 46410 (6505 Broadway Ave., 219-736-5633)
Indianapolis 46208 (3833 N. Meridian St., Suite 120, 317-927-6440)
National Cemeteries:
Crown Hill NC 46208 (700 W. 38th St., Indianapolis, 765-674-0284)
Marion NC 46952 (1700 E. 38th St., 765-674-0284)
New Albany NC 47150 (1943 Ekin Ave., 502-893-3852)

IOWA
Medical Centers:
Central Iowa HC System:
    #Des Moines 50310 (3600 30th St., 800-294-8387)
    #*Knoxville 50138 (1515 W. Pleasant St., 800-816-8878)
Iowa City 52246 (601 Hwy 6 West, 319-338-0581)
Clinics:
Bettendorf 52722 (2979 Victoria St., 563-332-8528)
Dubuque 52001 (200 Mercy Dr., Suite 106, 563-589-8899)
Fort Dodge 50501 (804 Kenyon Rd., Suite 160, 515-576-2235)
Mason City 50401 (910 N. Eisenhower, 641-421-8077 or 800-351-4671)
Sioux City 51104 (1551 Indian Hills Dr., Suite 206, 712-258-4700)
Waterloo 50701 (1015 S. Hackett Rd., 319-235-1235)
Regional Office:
Des Moines 50309 (210 Walnut St., Rm. 1063; statewide, 1-800-827-1000)
Vet Centers:
Cedar Rapids 52402 (1642 42nd St. N.E., 319-378-0016)
Des Moines 50310 (2600 Martin Luther King Jr. Pkwy., 515-284-4929)
Sioux City 51104 (1551 Indian Hills Dr., Suite 204, 712-255-3808)
National Cemetery:
Keokuk NC 52632 (1701 J St., 309-782-2094)

KANSAS
Medical Centers:
Eastern Kansas HC System:
    #*Leavenworth 66048 (4101 S. 4th St., Trafficway, 913-682-2000)
    *Topeka 66622 (2200 SW Gage Blvd., 785-350-3111)
*Wichita 67218 (5500 E. Kellogg, 316-685-2221)
Clinics:
Abilene 67410 (510 NE 10th St., 785-263-2100, ext. 161)
Chanute 66720 (629 S. Plummer, 620-431-4000, ext. 1553)

Fort Dodge City 67801 (300 Custer, 620-225-7146)
Emporia 66801 (12th and Chestnut, 620-434-6800, ext. 3351)
Fort Scott 66701 (710 W. 8th St., 620-223-8400)
Garnett 66032 (421 S. Maple, 785-448-3131, ext. 309)
Hays 67601 (207B E. 7th St., 785-625-3550)
Holton 66436 (1110 Columbine Dr., 785-364-2116, ext. 115)
Junction City 66441 (1102 St. Mary's Rd., 785-238-4131, ext. 4408)
Kansas City 66102 (21 N. 12th St., Ste. 200, 800-952-8387 ext. 6990)
Lawrence 66044 (404 Maine St., 785-842-3635)
Liberal 67901 (2 Rock Island Rd., Suite 200, 620-626-5574)
Paola 66071 (501 S. Hospital Dr., Suite 100, 816-922-2160)
Parsons 67357 (1401 Main, 620-423-3858)
Russell 67665 (200 South Main St., 785-483-3131, ext. 378)
Salem 65560 (P.O. Box 774, 573-729-6626)
Salina 67401 (1410 East Iron, Suite 1, 785-826-1580)
Seneca 66538 (1600 Community Dr., 785-336-6181, ext. 162)
Regional Office:
Wichita 67218 (5500 E. Kellogg Ave., 1-800-827-1000)
Vet Center:
Wichita 67211 (413 S. Pattie, 316-265-3260)
National Cemeteries:
Fort Leavenworth NC 66027 (913-758-4105)
Fort Scott NC 66701 (P.O. Box 917, 900 East Nat'l, 316-223-2840)
Leavenworth NC 66048 (P.O. Box 1694, 913-758-4105)

KENTUCKY
Medical Centers:
#* Ft. Thomas 41075 (1000 S. Ft. Thomas Ave., 513-861-3100)
*Lexington 40502-2236 (1101 Veterans Dr., 859-233-4511)
Louisville 40206 (800 Zorn Ave., 502-287-4000)
Clinics:
Bellevue 41073 (103 Landmark Dr., 859-392-3840)
Bowling Green 42103 (1110 Wilkinson Trace Cir., Harland, 270-796-3590)
Fort Campbell 42223 (Desert Storm Ave., Bldg. 61639, 270-798-4118)
Fort Knox 40121 (851 Ireland Loop, 502-624-9396)
Louisville/Dupont 40207 (4010 Dupont Circle, 502-287-6986)
Louisville/Shively 40216 (3934 N. Dixie Hwy, Suite 210, 502-287-6000)
Louisville/Standiford Field 40213 (1101 Grade Lane, 502-364-9635)
Paducah 42001 (1800 Clark St., 270-444-8465)
Prestonsburg 41653 (5230 KY Rt. 321, Suite 8, 606-886-1970)
Somerset 42501 (104 Hardin Lane, 606-676-0786)
Regional Office:
Louisville 40202 (545 S. Third St.; statewide, 1-800-827-1000)
Vet Centers:
Lexington 40507 (301 E. Vine St., Suite C, 859-253-0717)
Louisville 40208 (1347 S. 3rd St., 502-634-1916)
National Cemeteries:
Camp Nelson NC 40356 (6980 Danville Rd., Nicholasville, 859-885-5727)

Cave Hill NC 40204 (701 Baxter Ave., Louisville, 502-893-3852)
Danville NC 40442 (277 N. First St., 859-885-5727)
Lebanon NC 40033 (20 Hwy. 208, 502-893-3852)
Lexington NC 40508 (833 W. Main St., 859-885-5727)
Mill Springs NC 42544 (9044 West Hwy. 80, Nancy, 859-885-5727)
Zachary Taylor NC 40207 (4701 Brownsboro Rd., Louisville, 502-893-3852)

LOUISIANA
Medical Centers:
*Alexandria 71306 (P.O. Box 69004, 318-473-0010)
*New Orleans 70112 (1601 Perdido St., 504-568-0811)
Shreveport 71101 (510 E. Stoner Ave., 318-221-8411)
Clinics:
Baton Rouge 70806 (7968 Essen Park Ave., 225-761-6700)
Jennings 70546 (1907 Johnson St., 337-824-1000)
Monroe 71203 (250 DeSiard Plaza, 318-343-6100)
Lafayette 70501 (2100 Jefferson St. 337-261-0734)
Regional Office:
New Orleans 70113 (701 Loyola Ave., statewide, 1-800-827-1000)
Vet Centers:
Kenner 70062 (2200 Veterans Blvd., Suite 114, 504-464-4743)
Shreveport 71104 (2800 Youree Dr., Bldg. 1, Suite 105, 318-861-1776)
National Cemeteries:
Alexandria NC 71360 (209 E. Shamrock St., Pineville, 601-445-4981)
Baton Rouge NC 70806 (220 N. 19th St., 225-654-3767)
Port Hudson NC 70791 (20978 Port Hickey Rd., Zachary, 225-654-3767)

MAINE
Medical Center:
*Augusta 04330 (1 VA Center, 207-623-8411)
Regional Office:
Togus 04330 (1 VA Center; statewide, 1-800-827-1000)
Clinics:
Bangor 04401 (304 Hancock St., Suite 3B, 207-561-3600)
Calais 04619 (18 Palmer St., 207-454-7849)
Caribou 04736 (163 Van Buren Dr., Suite 6, 207-498-8785)
Rumford 04276 (209 Lincoln Ave., 207-364-4098)
Saco 04072 (655 Main St., 207-294-3100)
Vet Centers:
Bangor 04401 (352 Harlow St., 207-947-3391)
Caribou 04736 (456 York St., Irving Complex, 207-496-3900)
Lewiston 04240 (Pkwy Complex, 29 Westminster St., 207-783-0068)
Portland 04103 (475 Stevens Ave., 207-780-3584)
Springvale 04083 (628 Main St., 207-490-1513)
National Cemetery:
Togus NC 04330 (1 VA Center; 508-563-7113)

MARYLAND
Medical Centers:
Maryland HC System:
*Baltimore 21201 (10 N. Green St., 410-605-7000)
#Perry Point 21902 (Bldg. 5H, 410-642-2411)
Baltimore 21218 (Rehabilitation and Extended Care Ctr., 3900 Loch Raven Blvd., 410-605-7000)
Clinics:
Cambridge 21613 (830 Chesapeake Dr., 410-228-6243)
Charlotte Hall 20622 (29431 Charlotte Hall Rd., 310-884-7102)
Cumberland 21502 (710 Memorial Ave., 301-724-0061)
Fort Howard 21052 (9600 North Point Rd., 410-477-1800)
Glen Burnie 21061 (1406 South Crain Hwy., 410-590-4140)
Greenbelt 20770 (7525 Greenway Center Dr., T-4, 301-345-2463)
Hagerstown 21742 (1101 Opal Court, 301-665-1462)
Loch Raven 21218 (3901 The Alameda, 410-605-7650)
Pocomoke 21851 (101 Market St., 410-957-6718)
Regional Office:
Baltimore 21201 (31 Hopkins Plaza Federal Bldg., 1-800-827-1000)
Vet Centers:
Baltimore 21207 (6666 Security Blvd., Suite 2, 410-277-3600)
Cambridge 21613 (5510 West Shore Dr., 410-228-6305 ext. 4123)
Elkton 21921 (103 Chesapeake Blvd. Suite A, 410-392-4485)
Silver Spring 20910 (1015 Spring St., Suite 101, 301-589-1073)
National Cemeteries:
Annapolis NC 21401 (800 West St., 410-644-9695)
Baltimore NC 21228 (5501 Frederick Ave., 410-644-9696)
Loudon Park NC 21228 (3445 Frederick Ave., Baltimore, 410-644-9696)

MASSACHUSETTS
Medical Centers:
Bedford 01730 (200 Springs Rd., 1-800-838-6331 or 781-275-7500)
Boston 02130 (150 S. Huntington Ave., 617-232-9500)
Brockton 02301 (940 Belmont St., 508-583-4500)
*Northampton 01053-9764 (421 N. Main St., 413-584-4040)
West Roxbury 02132 (1400 VFW Pkwy., 617-323-7700)
Clinics:
Boston 02114 (251 Causeway St., 617-248-1000)
Dorchester 02124 (895 Blue Hill Ave., 617-822-7146)
Edgartown 02539 (55 Simpson's Lane, 508-627-1044)
Fitchburg 01420 (275 Nichols Rd., 978-342-9781)
Framingham 01702 (61 Lincoln St., 508-628-0205)
Franklin County 01301 (51 Sanderson St., Ste. 9, 413-773-8428)
Gloucester 01930 (298 Washington St., 978-282-0676)
Haverhill 01830 (108 Merrimack St., 978-372-5207)
Hyannis 02601 (145 Falmouth Rd., 508-771-3190)
Lowell 01852 (130 Marshall Rd., 978-671-9000)
Lynn 01904 (225 Boston St., Suite 107, 781-595-9818)

Martha's Vineyard Hospital 02557 (Linton Lane, Oak Bluffs, 508-693-0410)
Nantucket Cottage Hospital 02554 (57 Prospect St., 508-228-1200)
New Bedford 02740 (175 Elm St., 508-994-0217)
Pittsfield 01201 (73 Eagle St., 413-443-4857)
Quincy 02169 (114 Whitwell St., 2nd Floor, 617-376-2010)
Springfield 01104 (25 Bond St., 413-731-6000)
Worcester 01605 (605 Lincoln St., 508-856-0104)
Regional Office:
Boston 02114 (JFK Fed. Bldg., Gov. Ctr., Rm. 1265; 1-800-827-1000)
(Towns of Fall River & New Bedford, counties of Barnstable, Dukes, Nantucket, Bristol, part of Plymouth served by Providence, R.I., RO)
Vet Centers:
Boston 02215 (665 Beacon St., 617-424-0565)
Brockton 02401 (1041-L Pearl St., 508-580-2730)
Lowell 01852 (73 East Merrimack St., 978-453-1151)
New Bedford 02740 (468 North St., 508-999-6920)
Springfield 01103 (1985 Main St., Northgate Plaza, 413-737-5167)
Worcester 01605 (597 Lincoln St., 508-856-7428)
National Cemetery:
Massachusetts NC 02532 (Connery Ave., Bourne, 508-563-7113)

MICHIGAN
Medical Centers:
*Ann Arbor 48105 (2215 Fuller Rd., 734-769-7100)
*Battle Creek 49015 (5500 Armstrong Rd., 269-966-5600)
*Detroit 48201 (4646 John R. St., 313-576-1000)
*Iron Mountain 49801 (325 E. H St., 906-774-3300 or 1-800-215-8262 in Mich. and Wis.)
*Saginaw 48602 (1500 Weiss St., 989-497-2500)
Clinics:
Benton Harbor 49022 (115 Main St., 269-934-9123)
Flint 48532 (G-3267 Beecher Rd., 810-720-2913)
Gaylord 49735 (806 S. Otsego, 989-732-6555)
Grand Rapids 49505 (3019 Coit, N.E., 616-365-9575)
Hancock 49930-1495 (890 Campus Dr., 906-482-7762)
Ironwood 49938 (930 Cloverland Dr., 906-932-0032)
Lansing 48910 (MSU, 138 Service Dr., East Lansing, 517-432-4311)
Marquette 49855 (425 Fisher St., 906-226-4618)
Menominee 49858 (1101 11th Ave., Suite 2, 906-863-1286)
Muskegon 49442 (165 E. Apple Ave., Suite 201, 616-725-4105)
Oscoda 48750 (5671 Skeel Ave., Suite 4, 989-747-0026)
Pontiac 48342 (950 University Dr., 248-409-0585)
Sault Ste. Marie 49788 (16523 S. Watertower Dr., #1, 906-495-3030)
Traverse City 49684 (3271 Racquet Club Dr., 231-932-9720)
Yale 48097 (7470 Brockway Rd., 810-387-3211)
Regional Office:
Detroit 48226 (Patrick V. McNamara Federal Bldg., 477 Michigan Ave., Rm. 1400; 1-800-827-1000)

Vet Centers:
Dearborn 48124-3438 (2881 Monroe St., Suite 100, 313-277-1428)
Detroit 48201 (4161 Cass Ave., 313-831-6509)
Grand Rapids 49507 (1940 Eastern SE, 616-243-0385)
National Cemetery:
Fort Custer NC 49012 (15501 Dickman Rd., Augusta, 616-731-4164)

MINNESOTA
Medical Centers:
*Minneapolis 55417 (One Veterans Dr., 612-725-2000)
#*St. Cloud 56303 (4801 Veterans Dr., 320-252-1670)
Clinics:
Brainerd 56401 (1777 Hwy 18 East, 218-855-1115)
Fergus Falls 56537 (1821 North Park St., 218-739-1400)
Hibbing Area 55746, 4 sites (612-725-1991)
Mankato Area, 15 sites (612-725-1991)
Maplewood 55109 (2785 White Bear Ave., Suite 210, 651-290-3040)
Montevideo 56265 (1025 N. 13th St., 320-269-2222)
Rochester 55902 (1617 Skyline Dr., 507-252-0885)
South Central 55746 (612-725-1991)
Regional Office:
St. Paul 55111 (Bishop Henry Whipple Federal Bldg., 1 Federal Dr., state-wide, 1-800-827-1000. Counties of Becker, Beltrami, Clay, Clearwater, Kittson, Lake of the Woods, Mahnomen, Marshall, Norman, Otter Tail, Pennington, Polk, Red Lake, Roseau, Wilkin served by Fargo, N.D., RO)
Vet Centers:
Duluth 55802 (405 E. Superior St., 218-722-8654)
St. Paul 55114 (2480 University Ave., 651-644-4022)
National Cemetery:
Fort Snelling NC 55450-1199 (7601 34th Ave. So., Minn., 612-726-1127)

MISSISSIPPI
Medical Centers:
#*Biloxi 39531 (400 Veterans Ave., 228-523-5000)
*Jackson 39216 (1500 E. Woodrow Wilson Dr., 601-362-4471)
Clinics:
Byhalia 38611 (12 East Brunswick St., for information, call 901-523-8990)
Columbus 39702 (824 Alabama St., 662-244-0391)
Greenville 38703 (1502 S. Colorado St., 662-332-9872)
Hattiesburg 39401 (231 Methodist Blvd., 601-296-3530)
Kosciusko 39090 (332 Hwy. 12 W., 662-289-8089, ext. 3039)
Meridian 39301 (2103 13th St., 601-482-3275)
Natchez 39120 (46 Sgt. Prentiss Dr., 601-384-8207)
Smithville 38870 (3 sites, for information call 901-523-8990)
Regional Office:
Jackson 39216 (1600 E. Woodrow Wilson Ave., statewide 1-800-827-1000)
Vet Centers:
Biloxi 39531 (288 Veterans Ave., 228-388-9938 or 228-388-6923)

Jackson 39216 (1755 Lelia Dr., Suite 104, 601-965-5727)
National Cemeteries:
Biloxi NC 39535-4968 (P.O. Box 4968, 400 Veterans Ave., 228-388-6668)
Corinth NC 38834 (1551 Horton St., 901-386-8311)
Natchez NC 39120 (41 Cemetery Rd., 601-445-4981)

MISSOURI
Medical Centers:
*Columbia 65201 (800 Hospital Dr., 573-814-6000)
Kansas City 64128 (4801 Linwood Blvd., 816-861-4700)
*Poplar Bluff 63901 (1500 N. Westwood Blvd., 573-686-4151)
St. Louis 63106 (915 N. Grand Blvd., 314-652-4100)
*St. Louis 63125 (1 Jefferson Barracks Dr., 314-652-4100)
Clinics:
Belton 64012 (17140 Bel-Ray Place, 816-922-2161 or 816-318-0251)
Cape Girardeau 63701 (2420 Veterans Memorial Dr., 573-339-0909)
Camdenton 65020 (246RE Highway 54, 573-317-1150)
Cameron 64429 (1111 Euclid, 816-861-4700, ext. 54251, or 816-632-6010)
Farmington 63640 (715 Maple Valley Dr., 573-760-1365)
Ft. Leonard Wood 65473 (PO Box 1239, 126 Missouri Ave., 573-329-8305)
Kirksville 63501 (1108 East Patterson, Suite 9, 660-627-8387)
Mexico 65265 (One Veterans Dr., 573-581-9530)
Mt. Vernon 65712 (600 N. Main St., 417-466-0118 or 1-800-253-8387)
Nevada 64772 (322 Prewitt, 417-448-8905 or 816-922-2163)
St. Charles 63304 (7 Jason Court, 636-498-1113 or 314-286-6988)
St. James 65559 (620 N. Jefferson, 573-265-0448)
St. Joseph 64506 (1011B E. Saint Maartens Dr., 1-800-952-8387, ext. 6925)
St. Louis 63136 (10600 Lewis and Clark Blvd., 314-388-0470)
Warrensburg 64093 (1300 Veterans Rd., 660-747-3864)
West Plains 65775 (1211 Missouri Ave., 417-257-2454)
Regional Office:
St. Louis 63103 (400 South 18th St.; statewide, 1-800-827-1000)
Benefits Office:
Kansas City 64128 (4801 Linwood Blvd., 1-800-525-1483, ext. 2660)
Vet Centers:
Kansas City 64111 (3931 Main St., 816-753-1866)
St. Louis 63103 (2345 Pine St., 314-231-1260)
National Cemeteries:
Jefferson Barracks NC 63125 (2900 Sheridan Rd., St. Louis, 314-260-8720)
Jefferson City NC 65101 (1024 E. McCarty St., 314-260-8720)
Springfield NC 65804 (1702 E. Seminole St., 417-881-9499)

MONTANA
Medical Centers:
Montana HC System
   Fort Harrison 59636 (William St., off Hwy. 12 West, 406-442-6410)
   *Miles City 59301 (210 S. Winchester, 406-232-3060)

Clinics:
Anaconda 59711 (118 E. 7th St., 406-563-6090)
Billings 59102 (2345 King Ave. W., 406-651-2142)
Bozeman 59715 (300 N. Willson, Suite 703G, 406-522-8923)
Glasgow 59230 (621 3rd St., South, 406-228-3554)
Great Falls 59405 (1417-9th St. South, Suite 200, 406-761-0179)
Miles City 59301 (210 S. Winchester, 406-232-3060
Missoula 59801 (900 North Orange, Suite 206, 406-327-0912)
Sidney 59270 (216 14th Avenue SW, 406-488-2307)
Kalispell 59901 (66 Claremont St., Lower Level Suite B, 406-751-5980)
Regional Office:
Fort Harrison 59636 (1892 William St. off Hwy. 12 West, 1-800-827-1000)
Vet Centers:
Billings 59102 (1234 Avenue C, 406-657-6071)
Missoula 59802 (500 N. Higgins Ave., 406-721-4918)

NEBRASKA
Medical Centers:
VA Nebraska-Western Iowa HC System:
  *Grand Island 68803 (2201 N. Broadwell Ave., 1-800-451-5796)
  Omaha 68105 (4101 Woolworth Ave, 402-346-8800)
Clinics:
Alliance 69301 (524 Box Butte Ave., 308-762-8814 or 1-800-764-5370)
Gering (Scottsbluff) 69341 (2540 N. 10th St., 308-220-3930)
Lincoln 68510 (600 S. 70th St., 402-489-3802)
Norfolk 68701 (301 N. 27th St., 402-844-8022)
North Platte 69101 (600 East Francis, Suite 3, 800-451-8796)
Rushville 69360 (309 West 3rd St., 308-327-2302 or 1-800-764-5370)
Sidney 69162 (1116 10th Ave., 308-254-5475)
Scottsbluff 69341 (1441 E. 20th St., 308-220-3930 or 1-800-764-5370)
Regional Office:
Lincoln 68516 (5631 S. 48th St.; statewide, 1-800-827-1000)
Vet Centers:
Lincoln 68508 (920 L St., 402-476-9736)
Omaha 68131 (2428 Cuming St., 402-346-6735)
National Cemetery:
Fort McPherson NC 69151-1031 (12004 S. Spur 56A, Maxwell, 308-582-4433)

NEVADA
Medical Centers:
Las Vegas—Nellis Air Force Base, 89191 (Mike O'Callaghan Federal Hospital, 4700 N. Vegas Blvd., 702-653-2227)
*Reno 89502 (1000 Locust St., 1-888-838-6256)
Clinics:
Carson Valley 89423 (925 Ironwood St., #2102, 1-888-838-6256, ext. 4000)
Ely 89301 (6 Steptoe Circle, 775-289-2788, ext. 105)
Henderson 89014 (2920 N. Green Valley Pkwy., Suite 215, 702-456-3825)

Las Vegas 89036 (PO Box 360001, N. Las Vegas, 702-636-3000)
Las Vegas 89102 (Psychiatric, 1501 S. Arville, 702-259-4646)
Las Vegas 89032 (2455 W. Cheyenne Ave., 702-636-6375)
Las Vegas 89106 (901 Rancho Lane, 702-636-6370)
Las Vegas 89106 (Homeless Veterans, 405 N. Wilson, 702-386-3125)
Las Vegas 89118 (4420 W. Diablo Dr., 702-636-3000, ext. 4475)
Las Vegas 89106 (916 W. Owens Ave., 702-636-6380)
Las Vegas 89129 (2410 Fire Mesa St., 702-636-6320)
Las Vegas 89121 (4187 S Pecos Rd., 702-636-6350)
Las Vegas 89103 (3880 S. Jones Blvd., 702-636-6390)
Las Vegas 89030 (1841 E. Craig Rd., 702-636-3090)
Las Vegas 89106 (630 S. Rancho Rd., 702-636-6355)
Pahrump 89048 (2100 E. Calvada Blvd., 775-727-7535)
Regional Office:
Reno 89502 (1201 Terminal Way; statewide, 1-800-827-1000)
Benefits Office:
Las Vegas 89107 (4800 Alpine Pl., Suite 17, 1-800-827-1000)
Vet Centers:
Las Vegas 89503 (1040 E. Sahara Ave., 702-388-6369)
Reno 89503 (1155 W. 4th St., Suite 101, 775-323-1294)

NEW HAMPSHIRE
Medical Center:
*Manchester 03104 (718 Smyth Rd., 603-624-4366 or 1-800-892-8384)
Clinics:
Littleton 03561 (600 St. Johnsbury Rd., 603-444-9328)
Portsmouth 03803 (302 Newmarket St., Bldg. 15, 603-624-4366 ext. 5500)
Tilton 03276 (139 Winter St., 603-624-4366 ext. 5600 or 1-800-892-8384)
Wolfeboro 03894 (183 North Main St., 603-569-4336)
Conway 03818 (7 Greenwood Ave., 603-447-2555)
Regional Office:
Manchester 03101 (Norris Cotton Bldg., 275 Chestnut St., 1-800-827-1000)
Vet Center:
Manchester 03104 (103 Liberty St., 603-668-7060/61)

NEW JERSEY
Medical Centers:
New Jersey HC System:
    *East Orange 07018 (385 Tremont Ave., 973-676-1000)
    #*Lyons 07939 (151 Knollcroft Rd., 908-647-0180)
Clinics:
Brick 08724 (970 Rt. 70, 732-206-8900)
Cape May 08204 (U.S.C.G. Trng. Ctr., 1 Munro Ave., 609-898-8700)
Elizabeth 07206 (654 East Jersey St., 908-994-0120)
Ft. Dix 08640 (Marshall Hall, 8th & Alabama, 609-562-2999)
Hackensack 07601 (385 Prospect Ave., 201-487-1390)
Ft. Monmouth 07703 (Patterson Clinic, Stephenson Ave., Bldg. 1075, 732-532-4500)

Jersey City 07302 (115 Christopher Columbus Dr., 201-435-3055)
Morristown 07960 (340 West Hanover Ave., 973-539-9794)
Newark 07102 (20 Washington Place, 973-645-1441)
New Brunswick 08901 (317 George St., 732-729-0646)
Paterson 07503 (275 Getty Ave., 973-247-1666)
Trenton 08611 (171 Jersey St, Bldg. 36, 609-989-2355)
Turnersville 08096 (160 Fries Mill Rd., 856-262-4140)
Ventnor 08406 (6601 Ventnor Ave., Suite 16, 609-823-3122)
Vineland 08360 (520 Northwest Blvd., 856-692-2881)
Regional Office:
Newark 07102 (20 Washington Pl.; statewide, 1-800-827-1000. Philadelphia, PA Regional Office serves counties of Atlantic, Burlington, Camden, Cape May, Cumberland, Gloucester, Salem)
Vet Centers:
Jersey City 07302 (115 Christopher Columbus Dr., Suite 200, 973-645-2038)
Newark 07102 (157 Washington St., 973-645-5954)
Trenton 08611 (171 Jersey St., Bldg. 36, 609-989-2260)
Ventnor 08406 (6601 Ventnor Ave., Suite 105, 609-487-8387)
National Cemeteries:
Beverly NC 08010 (916 Bridgeboro Rd., 609-877-5460)
Finn's Point NC 08079 (Box 542, R.F.D. 3, Fort Mott Rd., Salem, 609-877-5460)

NEW MEXICO
Medical Center:
*Albuquerque 87108 (1501 San Pedro Dr., SE., 505-265-1711)
Clinics:
Alamogordo 88310 (1410 Aspen, 505-437-9195)
Artesia 88210 (1700 W. Main St., 505-746-3531)
Clovis 88101 (100 E. Manana St., Suite 1, 505-763-4335)
Espanola 87532 (620 Coronado St, Suite-B, 505-753-7395)
Farmington 87401 (1001 W. Broadway, Suite C, 505-326-4383)
Gallup 87301 (320 State Hwy., 564, 505-722-7234)
Hobbs 88240 (1601 N. Turner, 505-391-0354)
Las Cruces 88011 (1635 Don Roser, 505-522-1241)
Las Vegas 87701 (Hot Springs Blvd., 505-425-6788)
Raton 87740 (1275 S. 2nd St., 505-445-2391)
Santa Fe 87507 (2213 Brothers Rd., Suite 600, 505-986-8645)
Silver City 88061 (1302 32nd St., 505-538-2921)
Truth or Consequences 87901 (1960 N. Date St., 505-894-7662)
Regional Office:
Albuquerque 87102 (Dennis Chavez, 500 Gold Ave., S.W.; 1-800-827-1000)
Vet Centers:
Albuquerque 87104 (1600 Mountain Rd. N.W., 505-346-6562)
Farmington 87402 (4251 E. Main, Suite C, 505-327-9684)
Santa Fe 87505 (2209 Brothers Rd., Suite 110, 505-988-6562)
National Cemeteries:
Fort Bayard NC 88036 (P.O. Box 189, 915-564-0201)

Santa Fe NC 87501 (501 N. Guadalupe St., 505-988-6400)

NEW YORK
Medical Centers:
*Albany 12208 (113 Holland Ave., 518-626-5000)
#*Canandaigua 14424 (400 Fort Hill Ave., 585-393-7100)
#*Bath 14810 (76 Veterans Ave., 607-664-4000)
*Bronx 10468 (130 W. Kingsbridge Rd., 718-584-9000)
VA New York Harbor Healthcare System:
  #*Brooklyn 11209 (800 Poly Place, 718-836-6600)
  New York 10010 (423 East 23rd St. (1st Ave.), 212-686-7500)
  St. Albans 11425 (179 St. & Linden Blvd., 718-526-1000)
VA Hudson Valley Healthcare System:
  *Castle Point 12511 (845-831-2000)
  #*Montrose 10548 (2094 Albany Post Rd., Route 9A/PO Box 100, 914-737-4400)
Northport 11768 (79 Middleville Rd., 631-261-4400)
*Syracuse 13210 (800 Irving Ave., 315-425-4400)
Western New York HC System:
  *Batavia 14020 (222 Richmond Ave., 585-343-7500)
  *Buffalo 14215 (3495 Bailey Ave., 716-834-9200)

Clinics:
Auburn 13201 (17 Lansing St., 315-255-7002)
Bainbridge 13733 (109 N. Main St., 607-967-8590)
Binghamton 13001 (425 Robinson St., 607-772-9100)
Brooklyn 11201 (40th Flatbush Ave. Ext., 8th Floor, 718-439-4300)
Bronx 10459 (953 Southern Blvd, 718-741-4900)
Buffalo 14209 (1298 Main St., 716-551-3800)
Buffalo 14214 (2963 Main St., 716-834-881-5855)
Carmel 10512 (1875 Route 6-Warwick Savings Bank, 845-228-5291)
Carthage 13619 (3 Bridge St., 315-493-4180)
Catskill 12414 (159 Jefferson Heights, Green Medical Arts Bldg., Suite A102, 518-943-7515)
Cortland 13405 (1129 Commons Ave., 607-662-1517)
Clifton Park 12065 (1673 Route 9, 518-383-8506)
Dunkirk 14048 (325 Central Ave., 716-366-2122)
Elizabethtown 12932 (Community Hosp., Box 277 Park St., 518-873-3295)
Elmira 14901 (200 Madison Ave. 877-845-3247, ext. 44640)
Fonda 12068 (2623 State Hwy. 30A, 518-853-1247)
Glens Falls 12801 (84 Broad St., 518-798-6066)
Goshen 10924 (30 Hatfield Ln., Suite 204, 845-294-6927)
Islip 11751 (39 Nassau Ave., 631-581-5330)
Ithaca 14850 (10 Arrowwood Dr., 607-274-4680)
Jamestown 14701 (890 East 2nd St., 716-661-1448)
Kingston 12401 (63 Hurley Ave., 845-331-8322)
Lackawanna 14218 (227 Ridge Rd., 716-822-5944)
Lindenhurst 11757 (560 N. Delaware Ave., 631-884-1133)
Lockport 14304 (5875 S. Transit Rd., 716-433-2025)

Lynbrook 11563 (235 Merrick Rd., 516-887-3666)
Malone 12953 (183 Park St., 518-481-2545)
Massena 13662 (1 Hospital Dr., 315-769-4253)
Monticello 12701 (461 Broadway, 845-791-4936)
New City 10956 (Citi Bank Bldg., #400, 20 Squadron Blvd. 845-634-8942)
New York 10027 (Harlem Center, 55 W. 125th St., 11th Fl., 212-828-5265)
New York 10014 (Soho Center, 245 West Houston St., 212-337-2569)
New York 10011 (OSP Center, 437 W. 16th St., 212-462-4461)
Niagara Falls 14301 (229 Pine Ave., 1-800-223-4810)
Olean 14760 (623 Main St., 716-375-7555)
Patchogue 11772 (4 Phyllis Dr., 631-758-4419)
Plainview 11803 (1425 Old Country Rd., 516-694-6008)
Plattsburgh 12901 (43 Durkee St., Suite 300, 518-561-8310)
Port Jervis 12771 (150 Pike St. 845-856-5396)
Poughkeepsie 12603 (Freedom Park, 488 Freedom Plains Rd., Suite 120, 845-452-5151)
Riverhead 11901 (89 Hubbard Ave., 631-727-7171)
Rochester 14620 (465 Westfall Rd., 585-463-2600)
Rome 13441 (125 Brookley Road, Building 510, 315-334-7100)
Schenectady 12309 (1346 Gerling Ave., Niskayuna, 518-346-3334)
Sidney 13733 (109 Main St., 607-967-8590)
Staten Island 10304 (1150 South Ave., 3rd Floor, Suite 301, 718-761-2963)
Sunnyside/North Queens 11104 (41-03 Queens Blvd., 718-741-4800)
Troy 12180 (295 River St., 518-274-7707)
Warsaw 14569 (400 N. Main St., 585-786-2233)
Wellsville 14895 (15 Loder St., 585-596-2056)
Westhampton 11978 (150 Old Riverhead Rd., 631-898-0599)
White Plains 10601 (23 South Broadway, 914-421-1951)
Yonkers 10701 (124 New Main St., 914-375-8055)

Regional Offices:
Buffalo 14202 (Niagara Center, 130 S. Elmwood St.; 1-800-827-1000.
 Serves counties not served by New York City Regional Office.)
New York City 10014 (245 W. Houston St.; statewide, 1-800-827-1000.
 Serves counties of Albany, Bronx, Clinton, Columbia, Delaware, Dutchess, Essex, Franklin, Fulton, Greene, Hamilton, Kings, Montgomery, Nassau, New York, Orange, Otsego, Putnam, Queens, Rensselaer, Richmond, Rockland, Saratoga, Schenectady, Schoharie, Suffolk, Sullivan, Ulster, Warren, Washington, Westchester.)

Benefits Offices: Call 1-800-827-1000
Albany 12208 (113 Holland Ave.)
Rochester 14620 (465 Westfall Rd.)
Syracuse 13202 (344 W. Genesee St.)

Vet Centers:
Albany 12206 (875 Central Ave., 518-438-2505)
Babylon 11702 (116 West Main St., 631-661-3930)
Bronx 10458 (130 West Kingsbridge Rd., Rm. 7A-13, 718-367-3500)
Brooklyn 11201 (25 Chapel St., Suite 604, 718-330-2825)
Buffalo 14202 (564 Franklin St., 716-882-0505)

New York 10004 (32 Broadway, Suite 200, 212-742-9591)
New York 10027 (55 West 125th St., 212-426-2200)
Rochester 14620 (1867 Mt. Hope Ave., 585-232-5040)
Staten Island 10301 (150 Richmond Terrace, 718-816-4799)
Syracuse 13210 (716 E. Washington St., 315-478-7127)
White Plains 10601 (300 Hamilton Ave., 914-682-6251)
Woodhaven 11421 (75-10B 91st Ave., 718-296-2871)
National Cemeteries:
Bath NC 14810 (76 Veterans Ave., San Juan Ave., 607-664-4853)
Calverton NC 11933-1031 (210 Princeton Blvd., 631-727-5410/5770)
Cypress Hills NC 11208 (625 Jamaica Ave., Brooklyn, 631-454-4949)
Long Island NC 11735-1211 (2040 Wellwood Ave., Farmingdale, 631-454-4949)
Saratoga NC 12871-1721 (200 Duell Rd., Schuylerville, 518-581-9128)
Woodlawn NC 14901 (1825 Davis St., Elmira, 607-732-5411)

NORTH CAROLINA
Medical Centers:
*Asheville 28805 (1100 Tunnel Rd., 828-298-7911 or 1-800-932-6408)
*Durham 27705 (508 Fulton St., 919-286-0411)
*Fayetteville 28301 (2300 Ramsey St., 910-488-2120)
*Salisbury 28144 (1601 Brenner Ave., 704-638-9000)
Clinics:
Charlotte 28262 (Presbyterian Plaza, 8401 Medical Ctr. Dr., #350, 704-547-0020)
Greenville 27858 (800 Moye Blvd., 252-830-2149)
Jacksonville 28540 (1021 Hargett St., 910-219-1339)
Morehead City 28557 (5420 Highway 70, 252-240-2349)
Raleigh 27610 (23 Sunnybrook Rd., Suite 107, 919-212-0129)
Wilmington 28401 (1606 Physicians Dr., Suite 104, 910-362-8811)
Winston-Salem 27103 (190 Kimel Park Dr., 336-768-3296, ext. 1209/10)
Regional Office:
Winston-Salem 27155 (Federal Bldg., 251 N. Main St., 1-800-827-1000)
Vet Centers:
Charlotte 28202 (223 S. Brevard St., Suite 103, 704-333-6107)
Fayetteville 28311 (4140 Ramsey St., Suite 110, 910-488-6252)
Greensboro 27406 (2009 S. Elm-Eugene St., 336-333-5366)
Greenville 27858 (150 Arlington Blvd., Suite B, 252-355-7920)
Raleigh 27604 (1649 Old Louisburg Rd., 919-856-4616)
National Cemeteries:
New Bern NC 28560 (1711 National Ave., 252-637-2912)
Raleigh NC 27610-3335 (501 Rock Quarry Rd., 704-636-2661/4621)
Salisbury NC 28144 (202 Government Rd., 704-636-2661/4621)
Wilmington NC 28403 (2011 Market St., 252-637-2912)

NORTH DAKOTA
Medical Center:
*Fargo 58102 (2101 N. Elm St., 701-232-3241)

Clinics:
Bismarck 58503 (Gateway Mall, 2700 State St., Suite 5, 701-221-9169)
Grafton 58237 (West 6th St., 701-352-4594)
Minot 58705 (10 Missile Ave., 701-727-9800)
Regional Office:
Fargo 58102 (2101 Elm St., statewide, 1-800-827-1000)
Vet Centers:
Bismarck 58501 (1684 Capital Way, 701-224-9751)
Fargo 58103 (3310 Fiechtner Dr., Suite 100, 701-237-0942)
Minot 58701 (2041 3rd St. N.W., 701-852-0177)

OHIO
Medical Centers:
#*Brecksville 44141 (10000 Brecksville Rd., 440-526-3030)
*Chillicothe 45601 (17273 State Route 104, 740-773-1141)
#*Cincinnati 45220 (3200 Vine St., 513-861-3100)
Cleveland 44106, (10701 East Blvd., 216-791-3800)
#*Dayton 45428 (4100 W. 3rd St., 937-268-6511)
Clinics:
Akron 44319-1116 (55 W. Waterloo, 330-724-7715)
Ashtabula 44004 (1230 Lake Ave., 440-964-6454)
Athens 45701 (510 W. Union St., 740-593-7314)
Canton 44702 (733 Market Ave., S., 330-489-4600)
Cleveland/McCafferty 44113 (4242 Lorain Ave., 216-939-0699)
Columbus 43203 (543 Taylor Ave., 614-257-5200)
Cincinnati 45245 (Eastgate Bldg. 4355 Ferguson Dr., #270, 513-943-3680)
E. Liverpool 43920 (332 W. 6th St., 330-386-4303)
Grove City 43123 (1955 Ohio Dr., 614-257-5800)
Hamilton 45011 (1755C S. Erie Hwy., 513-870-9744)
Lancaster 43130 (Colonnade Med. Bldg, 1550 Sheridan Dr., 740-653-6145)
Lima 45804 (1303 Bellefontaine Ave., 419-222-5788)
Lorain 44052 (205 W. 20th St., 440-244-3833)
Mansfield 44906 (1456 Park Avenue West, 419-529-4602)
Marietta 45750 (418 Colegate Dr., 740-568-0412)
Marion 43302 (1203 Delaware Ave., 614-257-5920)
Middletown 45042 (675 N. University Blvd., 513-423-8387)
New Philadelphia 44663 (1260 Monroe Ave., 15H, 330-602-5339)
Painesville 44077 (W. 7 Jackson St., 440-357-6740)
Portsmouth 45662 (621 Broadway St., 740-353-3236)
Ravenna 44266 (6751 N. Chestnut St., 330-296-3641)
St. Clairsville 43950 (107 Plaza Dr., Suite 0, 740-695-9321)
Sandusky 44870 (3416 Columbus Ave., 419-625-7350)
Springfield 45505 (512 S. Burnett Rd., 937-328-3385)
Toledo 43614 (3333 Glendale Ave., 419-259-2000)
Warren 44485 (Riverside Sq., 1400 Tod Ave. NW, 330-392-0311)
Youngstown 44505 (2031 Belmont Ave., 330-740-9200)
Zanesville 43701 (840 Bethesda Dr., Bldg., 3-A, 740-453-7725)

Regional Office:
Cleveland 44199 (Anthony J. Celebrezze Bldg., 1240 E. 9th St., 1-800-827-1000)
Benefits Offices:
Cincinnati 45202 (36 E. Seventh St., Suite 210, 1-800-827-1000)
Columbus 43215 (Federal Bldg., Rm. 309, 200 N. High St., 1-800-827-1000)
Vet Centers:
Cincinnati 45203 (801-B W. 8th St., 513-763-3500)
Cleveland Heights 44118 (2022 Lee Rd., 216-932-8471)
Columbus 43215 (30 Spruce St., 614-257-5550)
Dayton 45402 (111 W 1st St., Suite 101, 937-461-9150)
Parma 44129 (5700 Pearl Rd., Suite 102, 440-845-5023)
National Cemeteries:
Dayton NC 45428-1008 (4100 W. Third St., 937-262-2115)
Ohio Western Reserve NC 44270 (P.O. Box 8, 10175 Rawiga Rd., Rittman, 330-335-3069)

OKLAHOMA
Medical Centers:
Muskogee 74401 (1011 Honor Heights Dr., 918-683-3261)
*Oklahoma City 73104 (921 N.E. 13th St., 405-270-0501)
Clinics:
Ardmore 73401 (1015 S. Commerce, 580-223-2266)
Clinton 73601 (1/4 mile south of I-40 on Highway 183, P.O. Box 1209)
Lawton/Ft. Sill 73503 (Bldg. 4303, 4303 Pittman and Thomas, 580-353-1131)
McAlester 74501 (903 E. Monroe St., 918-423-2880)
Ponca City 74647 (601 N.W. South St., 306 Fairview, 580-362-2555)
Seminole Co. 74849 (Konawa, 527 W. Third St., 580-925-3286)
Tulsa 74145 (9322 E. 41st St., 918-764-7243)
Regional Office:
Muskogee 74401 (Federal Bldg., 125 S. Main St., 1-800-827-1000)
Benefits Office:
Oklahoma City 73102 (Federal Cam., 301 NW 6th St., 113, 1-800-827-1000)
Vet Centers:
Oklahoma City 73105 (3033 N. Walnut, Suite 101W, 405-270-5184)
Tulsa 74112 (1408 S. Harvard, 918-748-5105)
National Cemetery:
Fort Gibson NC 74434 (1423 Cemetery Rd., 918-478-2334)
Fort Sill NC 73538 (2648 Jake Dunn Rd., 580-492-3200)

OREGON
Medical Centers:
#*Portland 97239 (3710 S.W. U.S. Veterans Hospital Rd., 503-220-8262)
*Roseburg 97470 (913 N.W. Garden Valley Blvd., 541-440-1000)
Clinics:
Bend 97701 (2115 Wyatt Court, Suite 201, 1-888-233-8305)
Bandon 97411 (1010 1st St. S.E., Suite 100, 541-347-4736)

Brookings 97415 (555 5th St., 541-412-1152)
Eugene 97404 (100 River Ave., 541-607-0897)
Klamath Falls 97601 (2819 Dahlia St, 541-273-6206/6129)
Salem 97301 (1660 Oak St., SE, 1-888-233-8305)
Warrenton 97146 (Camp Rilea, 91400 Rilea Neocoxie Rd., Bldg. 7315, 1-888-233-8305)
Rehabilitation Center:
White City 97503 (8495 Crater Lake Hwy., 541-826-2111, ext. 3210 or 3239)
Regional Office:
Portland 97204 (Federal Bldg., 1220 S.W. Third Ave., 1-800-827-1000)
Vet Centers:
Eugene 97403 (1255 Pearl St., 541-465-6918)
Grants Pass 97526 (211 S.E. 10th St., 541-479-6912)
Portland 97220 (8383 N.E. Sandy Blvd., Suite 110, 503-273-5370)
Salem 97301 (617 Chemeketa St., N.E., 503-362-9911)
National Cemeteries:
Eagle Point NC 97524 (2763 Riley Rd., 541-826-2511)
Roseburg NC 97470 (913 Garden Valley Blvd, 541-826-2511)
Willamette NC 97266-6937 (11800 S.E. Mt. Scott Blvd., Portland, 503-273-5250)

PENNSYLVANIA
Medical Centers:
*Altoona 16602 (2907 Pleasant Valley Blvd., 814-943-8164)
#*Butler 16001 (325 New Castle Rd., 724-287-4781 or 800-362-8262)
#*Coatesville 19320 (1400 Black Horse Hill Rd., 610-384-7711)
*Erie 16504-1596 (135 E. 38th St., 814-868-8661 or 800-274-8387)
*Lebanon 17042 (1700 S. Lincoln Ave., toll free 1-800-409-8771)
*Philadelphia 19104 (University & Woodland Aves., 1-800-949-1001)
Pittsburgh HC System:
 Pittsburgh 15240 (University Dr., 412-688-6000 or 1-866-482-7488)
*Wilkes-Barre 18711 (1111 East End Blvd., 570-824-3521)
Clinics:
Aliquippa 15001 (2360 Hospital Dr., 724-857-0424)
Allentown 18103 (3100 Hamilton Blvd., 610-776-4304 or 1-866-249-6472)
Berwick 18603 (301 West 3rd St., 570-759-0351)
Camp Hill 17011 (25 N. 23rd St., 717-730-9782)
DuBois 15801 (190 West Park Ave., Suite B, 814-375-6817)
Ellwood City 16117 (Medical Arts Bldg., 304 Evans Dr., 724-285-2203)
Farrell 16121 (Primary Health Network, 602 Roemer Blvd., 724-285-2216)
Frackville 17931 (10 East Spruce St., 570-874-4289)
Greensburg 15601 (Hempfield Plaza, Rt. 30, 724-837-5200)
Johnstown 15904 (University Park, 1425 Scalp Ave., #29, 814-266-8696)
Kittanning 16201 (ACMH, 1 Nolte Dr., Suite 130, 724-542-8711)
Knox 16232 (Houston Family Health, 400 Huston Ave., 814-797-1276)
Lancaster 17601 (Greenfield, 1861 Charter Lane, #118, 717-290-6900)
Meadville 16335 (18955 Park Avenue Plaza, 814-337-0170)
New Castle 16101 (Jameson South, 1000 S. Mercer St., 724-285-2203)

Pottsville 17901 (Schuykill Co., GSH Reg. Med. Ctr., 700 E. Norwegian St., 570-621-4561)
Reading 19601 (145 N. Sixth St., 3rd Fl., St. Jos., 610-208-4719)
Sayre 18840 (301 N. Elmira, 570-888-6803 or 1-877-470-0920)
Shippenville 16254 (Marianne Family, 21159 Paint Blvd., #2, 814-226-6770)
State College 16801-2755 (3048 Enterprise Dr., Ferguson Square, Bldg., 1, 814-867-5415)
Schuylkill Haven 17972 (Rt. 61 S. Greenview Rd., 570-366-3915)
Smethport 16749 (406 Franklin St, 814-887-5655)
Spring City 19475 (11 Independence Dr., 610-948-1082)
Springfield 19064 (194 W. Sproul Rd., Crozier Keystone, 610-543-3246)
Tobyhanna 18466 (Bldg. 220, Army Depot, 570-895-8341)
Washington County 15301 (100 Ridge Ave., 724-250-7790)
Williamsport 17701 (Divine Providence, #304, 1705 Warren Ave., 570-322-4791)
Willow Grove/Horsham 19044 (433 Caredean, 215-823-6050)
York 17403 (1796 3rd Ave., 717-854-2481)
Regional Offices:
Philadelphia 19101 (RO and Insurance Center, P.O. Box 8079, 5000 Wissahickon Ave., RO, 1-800-827-1000. Serves counties of Adams, Berks, Bradford, Bucks, Cameron, Carbon, Centre, Chester, Clinton, Columbia, Dauphin, Delaware, Franklin, Juniata, Lackawanna, Lancaster, Lebanon, Lehigh, Luzerne, Lycoming, Mifflin, Monroe, Montgomery, Montour, Northampton, Northumberland, Perry, Philadelphia, Pike, Potter, Schuylkill, Snyder, Sullivan, Susquehanna, Tioga, Union, Wayne, Wyoming, York.)
Pittsburgh 15222 (1000 Liberty Ave.; statewide, 1-800-827-1000. Serves remaining counties of Pennsylvania.)
Benefits Office:
Wilkes-Barre 18711 (111 East End Blvd., Bldg. 17, #110, 1-800-827-1000)
Vet Centers:
Erie 16501 (1000 State St., Suite 1&2, 814-453-7955)
Harrisburg 17102 (1500 N. 2nd St., Suite 2, 717-782-3954)
McKeesport 15131 (2001 Lincoln Way., 412-678-7704)
Philadelphia 19107 (801 Arch St., Suite 102, 215-627-0238)
Philadelphia 19120 (101 E. Olney Ave., 215-924-4670)
Pittsburgh 15205 (2500 Baldwick Rd., Suite 15, 412-920-1765)
Scranton 18505 (1002 Pittston Ave., 570-344-2676)
Williamsport 17701 (805 Penn St., 570-327-5281)
National Cemeteries:
Indiantown Gap NC 17003-9618 (R.R. 2, P.O. Box 484, Annville, 717-865-5254)
Philadelphia NC 19138 (Haines St. & Limekiln Pike, 609-877-5460)

PHILIPPINES
Regional Office:
Manila 0930 (1131 Roxas Blvd., 011-632-528-6300, International Mailing Address: PSC 501, FPO AP 96515-1100)

Clinic:
Manila (2201 Roxas Blvd., Pasay City, 1300 Philippines, 011-632-833-4566, International Mailing Address same as above)

PUERTO RICO
Medical Center:
*San Juan 00921-3201 (10 Casia St., 787-641-7582 or 1-800-449-8729)
Clinics:
Arecibo 00612 (Calle Gonzalo Marín #50, 787-816-1818 or 1-866-874-6569)
Guayama 00784 (FISA Building-First Floor, Paseo del Pueblo, Km. 0.3, Lote No. 6, 787-866-8886)
Mayaguez 00680-1507 (Ave. Hostos 345, 787-834-6900)
Ponce 00716-2001 (10 Paseo del Veterano, 787-812-3030)
Regional Office:
San Juan 00918-1703 (150 Carlos Chardon Ave., Suite 300. Send mail to Suite 232. Serving all Puerto Rico and the Virgin Islands, 1-800-827-1000)
Benefits Offices: Call 1-800-827-1000
Mayaguez 00680-1507 (Ave. Hostos 345, Carretera 2, Frente Medico)
Ponce 00731 (10 Paseo del Veterano)
Arecibo 00612 (Gonzalo Marin #50)
San Juan 00921-3201 (VAMC, 10 Calle Casia)
Vet Centers:
Arecibo 00612-4702 (52 Gonzalo Marin St., 787-879-4510/4581)
Ponce 00731 (35 Mayo St., 787-841-3260)
San Juan 00921 (Condominio Med. Ctr. Plaza, Suite LC8A11, La Riviera, 787-749-4409)
National Cemetery:
Puerto Rico NC 00960 (Avenue Cementerio Nacional #50, Barrio Hato Tejas, Bayamon, 787-798-7620)

RHODE ISLAND
Medical Center:
Providence 02908 (830 Chalkstone Ave., 401-273-7100)
Clinic:
Middletown 02842 (One Corporate Pl., West Main Rd., 401-847-6239)
Regional Office:
Providence 02903 (380 Westminster St.; statewide, 1-800-827-1000)
Vet Center:
Warwick 02889 (2038 Warwick Ave., 401-739-0167)

SOUTH CAROLINA
Medical Centers:
*Charleston 29401 (109 Bee St., 843-577-5011)
*Columbia 29209-1639 (6439 Garners Ferry Rd., 803-776-4000)
Clinics:
Anderson 29621 (1702 East Greenville St., 864-224-5450)
Beaufort 29902 (1 Pinckney Blvd., 843-770-0444)

Florence 29501 (1805 Pamplico Highway, Medical Mall A, Suite 220A, 843-292-8383)
Greenville 29605 (3510 Augusta Rd., 864-299-1600)
Myrtle Beach 29577 (3381 Phillis Blvd., 843-477-0177)
Rock Hill 29732-1817 (124 Glenwood Dr., 803-328-3622)
Sumter 29150 (407 N. Salem St., 803-938-9901)
Orangeburg 29118 (1767 Village Park Dr., 803-533-1335)
Regional Office:
Columbia 29201 (1801 Assembly St.; statewide, 1-800-827-1000)
Vet Centers:
Columbia 29201 (1513 Pickens St., 803-765-9944)
Greenville 29601 (14 Lavinia Ave., 864-271-2711)
North Charleston 29406 (5603-A Rivers Ave., 843-747-8387)
National Cemeteries:
Beaufort NC 29902-3947 (1601 Boundary St., 843-524-3925)
Florence NC 29501 (803 E. National Cemetery Rd., 843-669-8783)

SOUTH DAKOTA
Medical Centers:
Black Hills HC System:
   *Fort Meade 57741 (113 Comanche Rd., 605-347-2511)
   #Hot Springs 57747 (500 N. 5th St., 605-745-2000 or 1-800-764-5370)
*Sioux Falls 57105 (2501 W. 22nd St., 605-336-3230)
Clinics:
Aberdeen 57401 (1440 15th Ave., NW, 605-622-2640)
Eagle Butte 57625 (15 Main St., 605-964-8000)
Isabel 57633 (118 N. Main St., 605-466-2120)
Faith 57626 (112 N. 2nd Ave., 605-967-2644)
Mission/Rosebud 57570 (Mission Medical Clinic, 605-856-2295)
Pierre 57501 (1601 N. Harrison, Suite 1A, 605-945-1710)
Rapid City 57701 (3625 5th St., 605-718-1095 or 1-800-743-1070)
Winner 57580 (915 E. 8th St., 605-842-2243)
McLauglin 57642 (Silver Barn Rd., 605-823-4574 or 1-800-743-1070)
Regional Office:
Sioux Falls 57117 (P.O. Box 5046, 2501 W. 22nd St.; 1-800-827-1000)
Vet Centers:
Martin 57551 (East Hwy 18, 605-685-1300)
Rapid City 57701 (621 6th St., Suite 101, Kansas City St., 605-348-0077)
Sioux Falls 57104 (601 S. Cliff Ave., Suite C, 605-330-4552)
National Cemeteries:
Black Hills NC 57785 (20901 Pleasant Valley Dr., Sturgis, 605-347-3830/7299)
Fort Meade NC 57785 (P.O. Box 640, Old Stone Rd., Sturgis, 605-347-3830/7299)
Hot Springs NC 57747 (500 N 5th St., 605-347-3830/7299)

TENNESSEE
Medical Centers:
*Memphis 38104 (1030 Jefferson Ave., 901-523-8990)
#*Mountain Home 37684 (P.O. Box 4000, 423-926-1171)
VA Tennessee Valley Healthcare System:
  Nashville 37212 (1310 24th Ave., South, 615-327-4751)
  Murfreesboro 37129 (3400 Lebanon Pike, 615-867-6000)
Clinics:
Chattanooga 37411 (150 Debra Rd., Suite 5200, Bldg 6200, 423-893-6500)
Clarksville 37043 (Gateway Ctr., #110, 1731 Memorial St., 931-221-2171)
Confington 38128 (3461 Austin Peay Hwy., 901-261-4500)
Cookeville 38501 (Primary Care, 1101 Neal St., 931-525-1653)
Dover 37058-0497 (1021 Spring St., PO Box 497, 931-232-5329)
Knoxville 37923 (9031 Cross Park Dr., 865-545-4592)
Memphis South 38116 (1056 East Raines Rd., 901-271-4900)
Mountain City 37683 (PO Box 738, 423-727-1103)
Nashville/Vine Hill 37204 (601 Benton Ave., 615-292-9770)
Rogersville 37857 (PO Box 850, 423-272-5600)
Savannah 38372 (150 East End Dr., 901-523-8990)
Tullahoma 37389 (225 First St., Arnold AFB, 931-454-6134)
Regional Office:
Nashville 37203 (110 9th Ave. South; statewide, 1-800-827-1000)
Vet Centers:
Chattanooga 37411 (951 Eastgate Loop Rd., 5700, #300, 423-855-6570)
Johnson City 37604 (1615A W. Market St., 423-928-8387)
Knoxville 37914 (2817 E. Magnolia Ave., 423-545-4680)
Memphis 38104 (1835 Union, Suite 100, 901-544-0173)
National Cemeteries:
Chattanooga NC 37404 (1200 Bailey Ave., 423-855-6590)
Knoxville NC 37917 (939 Tyson St., N.W., 423-855-6590)
Memphis NC 38122 (3568 Townes Ave., 901-386-8311)
Mountain Home NC 37684 (P.O. Box 8, VAMC, Bldg. 117, 423-979-3535)
Nashville NC 37115-4619 (1420 Gallatin Rd. So., Madison, 615-736-2839)

TEXAS
Medical Centers:
*Amarillo 79106 (6010 Amarillo Blvd., West, 806-355-9703)
*Houston 77030 (2002 Holcombe Blvd., 713-791-1414)
*Big Spring 79720 (300 Veterans Blvd., 800-472-1365)
Central Texas HC System
  #*Temple 76504 (1901 Veterans Mem., Dr., 800-423-2111, 254-778-4811)
  Waco 76711 (4800 Memorial Dr., 254-752-6581 or 1-800-423-2111)
North Texas HC System
  #*Bonham 75418 (1201 East Ninth St., 800-924-8387)
  #*Dallas 75216 (4500 S. Lancaster Rd., 800-849-3597)
South Texas HC System
  *San Antonio 78229-4404 (7400 Merton Minter Blvd., 210-617-5300)
  *Kerrville 78028 (3600 Memorial Blvd., 830-896-2020)

Clinics:
Abilene 78606 (4225 Woods Place, 325-695-3252)
Alice 78384 (215 Dr. E.E. Dunlap St. 361-279-3378)
Austin 78741 (2901 Montopolis Dr., 512-389-1010)
Beaumont 77707 (3420 Veteran Circle, 409-981-8550)
Beeville 78102 (302 South Hillside Dr., 361-358-9912)
Bonham/Red River (Grayson, Delta, and Lamar Counties, 800-924-8387, ext. 36676 or 903-583-6676)
Brownsville 78520 (394 Military Hwy., 956-544-3226 or 956-546-5194)
Brownwood 76801 (2600 Memorial Park Dr., 325-641-0568)
Cedar Park 78613 (701 E. Whitestone Blvd., 512-260-1368)
Childress 79201 (Highway 83 North, 940-937-3636)
Cleburne (Johnson and Ellis Counties, 800-849-3597 ext. 71465)
College Station/Bryan 77845 (1605 Rock Prairie Rd., #212, 979-680-0361)
Corpus Christi 78405 (5283 Old Brownsville Rd., 361-806-5600)
Decatur 76426 (Wise, Jack, Clay, Archer, Baylor, Young, Throckmorton and Montague Counties, 800-849-3597 ext. 36342 or 214-857-1465)
Denton 76201 (Denton, Cooke and Collin Counties, 800-924-8387, ext. 36676 or 903-583-6676)
Eastland (Eastland, Parker, Palo Pinto, Hood, Callahan and Stephens Counties, 800-849-3597 ext. 71465 or 214-857-1465)
El Paso 79930 (5001 N. Piedras St., 915-564-6100)
Fort Stockton 79735 (Sanderson Hwy., 915-336-8365)
Fort Worth 76104 (300 W. Rosedale St., 800-443-9672)
Greenville (Kaufman, Hopkins, Hunt, Rockwall, Titus and Franklin Counties, 800-849-3597 ext. 71465 or 214-857-1465)
Harlingen 78550 (1629 Treasure Hills Blvd., 956-366-4500)
Kingsville 78343 (301 West Main, 361-584-2563)
Laredo 78041 (6551 Star Ct., 956-523-7850)
Longview 75601 (1205 E. Marshall Ave., 903-247-8262)
Lubbock 79412 (6104 Ave., Q South Dr., 806-472-3400)
Lufkin 75904 (1301 W. Frank Ave., 936-637-1342)
Marlin 76661 (1016 Ward St., 254-883-3511 or 1-800-423-2111)
McAllen 78503 (2101 S. Colonel Rowe Blvd., 956-618-7103)
McAllen/Family Medical-UT 78503 (205 East Toronto, 956-687-6155)
New Braunfels 78130 (189 E. Austin St., Suite 106)
Odessa 79761 (419 W. Fourth St., 432-580-4560)
Palestine 75801 (2000 S. Loop 256, Suite 200, 903-723-9006)
Red River Co. 75462 (800-924-8387 ext. 36342 or 903-583-6342)
San Angelo 76905 (2018 Pulliam, 325-658-6138)
San Antonio 78240 (5788 Eckert Rd., 210-699-2100)
San Antonio/General 78226 (1831 General McMullen, 210-434-1400)
San Antonio/Greenway 78217 (2455 NE Loop 410, #100, 210-599-6000)
San Antonio/N. Hills 78217 (13909 Nacogdoches, #124, 210-653-8989)
San Antonio/NW 78229 (4600 NW Loop 410, Suite 110, 210-280-0040)
San Antonio/Pecan Valley 78222 (4243 E. Southcross, #205, 210-304-3500)
South Bexar Co. 78223 (1055 Ada, San Antonio, 210-358-5701)
Stamford 79553 (1303 Mabee Dr., 325-773-5733)

Stratford 79084 (1220 Purnell St., 806-396-5583)
Tarrant Co. 76107 (call 800-924-8387 ext. 36676 or 903-583-6676)
Tyler 75701 (Smith, Camp, Henderson, Van Zandt, Rains and Wood Counties, call 800-849-3597 ext. 71465 or 214-857-1465)
Uvalde 78801 (1025 Garner Field Rd., 830-278-1692)
Victoria 77901 (1502 E. Airline, Suite 40, 361-582-7700)
Wichita Falls 76301 (1800 7th St., 940-723-2373)

Regional Offices:

Houston 77030 (6900 Almeda Rd., statewide, 1-800-827-1000. Serves counties of Angelina, Aransas, Atacosa, Austin, Bandera, Bee, Bexar, Blanco, Brazoria, Brewster, Brooks, Caldwell, Calhoun, Cameron, Chambers, Colorado, Comal, Crockett, DeWitt, Dimitt, Duval, Edwards, Fort Bend, Frio, Galveston, Gillespie, Goliad, Gonzales, Grimes, Guadeloupe, Hardin, Harris, Hays, Hidalgo, Houston, Jackson, Jasper, Jefferson, Jim Hogg, Jim Wells, Karnes, Kendall, Kennedy, Kerr, Kimble, Kinney, Kleberg, LaSalle, Lavaca, Liberty, Live Oak, McCulloch, McMullen, Mason, Matagorda, Maverlck, Medina, Menard, Montgomery, Nacogdoches, Newton, Nueces, Orange, Pecos, Polk, Real, Refugio, Sabine, San Augustine, San Jacinto, San Patricio, Schleicher, Shelby, Starr, Sutton, Terrell, Trinity, Tyler, Uvalde, Val Verde, Victoria, Walker, Waller, Washington, Webb, Wharton, Willacy, Wilson, Zapata, Zavala)

Waco 76799 (One Veterans Plaza, 701 Clay; statewide, 1-800-827-1000; serves the rest of the state. In Bowie County, the City of Texarkana is served by Little Rock, AR, RO, 1-800-827-1000.)

Benefits Offices: *Call 1-800-827-1000*

Abilene 79602 (Taylor County Bldg., 103, 400 Oak St.)
Amarillo 79106 (6010 Amarillo Blvd. W.)
Austin 78741 (2901 Montopolis Dr., Room 108)
Corpus Christi 78405 (4646 Corona Dr., Suite 150)
Dallas 75216 (4500 S. Lancaster Rd.)
El Paso 79930 (5001 Piedras Dr.)
Ft. Worth 76104-4856 (300 W. Rosedale St.)
Lubbock 79410 (4902 34th St., Suite 10, Rm. 134)
McAllen 78503 (1901 South 1st St., Suite 400)
San Antonio 78240 (5788 Eckert Rd.)
Temple 76504 (1901 Veterans Mem. Dr., Rm. 5G38 [BRB])
Tyler 75701 (1700 SSE Loop 323, Suite 310)

Vet Centers:

Amarillo 79109 (3414 Olsen Blvd., Suite E., 806-354-9779)
Austin 78745 (1110 W. Will Cannon Dr., Suite 301, 512-416-1314)
Corpus Christi 78411 (4646 Corona, Suite 250, 361-854-9961)
Dallas 75244 (5232 Forest Lane, Suite 111, 214-361-5896)
El Paso 79925 (1155 Westmoreland, Suite 121, 915-772-0013)
Fort Worth 76104 (1305 W. Magnolia, Suite B, 817-921-9095)
Houston 77006 (503 Westheimer, 713-523-0884)
Houston 77024 (701 N. Post Oak Rd., Suite 102, 713-682-2288)
Laredo 78041 (6020 McPherson Rd., #1A, 956-723-4680)
Lubbock 79410 (3208 34th St., 806-792-9782)

McAllen 78504 (801 Nolana, Suite 140, 956-631-2147)
Midland 79703 (3404 W. Illinois, Suite 1, 915-697-8222)
San Antonio 78212 (231 W. Cypress St. Suite 100, 210-472-4025)
National Cemeteries:
Dallas-Fort Worth NC 75211 (2000 Mountain Creek Parkway, 214-467-3374)
Fort Bliss NC 79906 (Box 6342, 5200 Fred Wilson Rd., 915-564-0201)
Fort Sam Houston NC 78209 (1520 Harry Wurzbach Rd., San Antonio, 210-820-3891/3894)
Houston NC 77038 (10410 Veterans Memorial Dr., 281-447-8686/0580)
Kerrville NC 78028 (VAMC, 3600 Memorial Blvd., 210-820-3891/3894)
San Antonio NC 78202 (517 Paso Hondo St., 210-820-3891/3894)

UTAH
Medical Center:
Salt Lake City 84148 (500 Foothill Drive, 801-582-1565)
Clinics:
Fountain Green 84632 (300 W. 300 S., 435-623-3129, ext. 2975)
Nephi 84648 (48 W. 1500 N., 435-623-3129. ext. 2975)
Ogden 84403 (982 Chambers St., 801-479-4105)
Orem 84057 (Timpanogos Med. Off. Bldg., 740 W. 800 North, Suite 440, 4th Floor, 801- 235-0953)
Roosevelt 84066 (210 West 300 North (75-3), 435-722-3971)
St. George 84770 (1067 E. Tabernacle, 435-634-7608)
Regional Office:
Salt Lake City 84158 (P.O. Box 581900, 550 Foothill Dr., 1-800-827-1000)
Vet Centers:
Provo 84601 (750 North 200 West, Suite 105, 801-377-1117)
Salt Lake City 84106 (1354 East 3300 South, 801-584-1294)

VERMONT
Medical Center:
White River Junction 05009 (215 N. Main St., 802-295-9363)
Clinics:
Bennington 05201 (Vermont Veterans Home, 325 North St., 802-447-6913)
Colchester 05446 (162 Hegeman Ave., 100, Ft. Ethan Allen, 802-655-1356)
Rutland 05702 (215 Stratton Rd., 802-773-3386)
Regional Office:
White River Junction 05009 (215 N. Main St., 802-296-5177, or 1-800-827-1000 from within Vermont)
Vet Centers:
South Burlington 05401 (359 Dorset St., 802-862-1806)
White River Junction 05001 (Gilman Office Complex #2, 222 Holiday Inn Dr., 802-295-2908 or 1-800-649-6603)

VIRGINIA
Medical Centers:
#*Hampton 23667 (100 Emancipation Dr., 757-722-9961)
*Richmond 23249 (1201 Broad Rock Blvd., 804-675-5000)

*Salem 24153 (1970 Roanoke Blvd., 540-982-2463)
Clinics:
Alexandria 22309 (8796 D Sacramento Dr., 703-719-6797)
Danville 24541 (Southside Medical, 2811 Riverside Dr., 434-799-1200)
Fredericksburg 22401 (1965 Jeff. Davis Hwy., 540-370-4468)
Harrisonburg 22802 (101 N. Main St., #220 Harrison Plaza, 540-442-1773)
Norton 24273 (Third St. N.E., 540-679-9107)
Stephens City 22655 (106 Hyde Ct., 540-869-0600)
Tazewell 24651 (Tazewell Physicians, 123 Ben Holt Ave. 276-988-2526)
Regional Office:
Roanoke 24011 (210 Franklin Rd., S.W.; statewide, 1-800-827-1000)
Vet Centers:
Alexandria 22309 (8796 Sacramento Dr., Suite D&E, 703-360-8633)
Norfolk 23517 (2200 Colonial Ave., Suite 3, 757-623-7584)
Richmond 23230 (4202 Fitzhugh Ave., 804-353-8958)
Roanoke 24016 (350 Albemarle Ave., SW, 540-342-9726)
National Cemeteries:
Alexandria NC 22314 (1450 Wilkes St., 703-221-2183/2184)
Balls Bluff NC 22075 (Rte. 7, Leesburg, 540-825-0027)
City Point NC 23860 (10th Ave. & Davis St., Hopewell, 804-795-2031)
Cold Harbor NC 23111 (Rt. 156 North, Mechanicsville, 804-795-2031)
Culpeper NC 22701 (305 U.S. Ave., 540-825-0027)
Danville NC 24541 (721 Lee St., 704-636-2661/4621)
Fort Harrison NC 23231 (8620 Varina Rd., Richmond, 804-795-2031)
Glendale NC 23231 (8301 Willis Church Rd., Richmond, 804-795-2031)
Hampton NC 23667 (Cemetery Rd. at Marshall Ave., 757-723-7104)
Hampton NC 23667 (VAMC, Emancipation Dr., 757-723-7104)
Quantico NC 22172 (P.O. Box 10, 18424 Joplin Rd. (Rte. 619), 703-221-2183/2184)
Richmond NC 23231 (1701 Williamsburg Rd., 804-795-2031)
Seven Pines NC 23150 (400 E. Williamsburg Rd., Sandston, 804-795-2031)
Staunton NC, 24401 (901 Richmond Ave., 540-825-0027)
Winchester NC 22601 (401 National Ave., 540-825-0027)

VIRGIN ISLANDS
Clinics:
St. Croix 00850-4701 (The Village Mall, 113, RR2 Box 10556, Kingshill, 340-778-5553)
St. Thomas 00802 (Buchaneer Mall, 8, 340-774-6674)
Benefits:
Served by San Juan, Puerto Rico, VA Regional Office, 1-800-827-1000
Vet Centers:
St. Croix 00850 (Box 12, R.R. 02, Village Mall, 113, RR2 Box 10556, Kingshill, 340-778-5553)
St. Thomas 00802 (9800 Buchaneer Mall, Suite 8, 340-774-6674)

WASHINGTON
Medical Centers:
Puget Sound HC System:
 *Seattle 98108 (1660 S. Columbian Way, 206-762-1010)
 #*Tacoma 98493 (9600 Veterans Dr., S.W., American Lake, 253-582-8440)
*Spokane 99205 (4815 N. Assembly St., 509-434-7000)
*Walla Walla 99362 (77 Wainwright Dr., 509-525-5200)
Clinics:
Bremerton 98310 (925 Adele Ave., 360-782-0129)
Tri-Cities 99352 (Richland, 948 Stevens Dr., Suite C, 509-946-1020)
Yakima 98902 (717 Fruitvale Blvd., 509-966-0199)
Regional Office:
Seattle 98174 (Fed. Bldg., 915 2nd Ave.; statewide, 1-800-827-1000)
Benefits Offices:
Fort Lewis 98433 (Waller Hall Rm. 700, P.O. Box 331153, 253-967-7106)
Bremerton 98337 (West Sound Pre-Separation Center, 262 Burwell St.)
Vet Centers:
Bellingham 98226 (3800 Byron Ave., Suite 124, 360-733-9226)
Seattle 98121 (2030 9th Ave., Suite 210, 206-553-2706)
Spokane 99206 (100 N. Mullan Rd., Suite 102, 509-444-8387)
Tacoma 98409 (4916 Center St., Suite E, 253-565-7038)
Yakima 98902 (1111 N. First St., 509-457-2736)
National Cemetery:
Tahoma NC 98042-4868 (18600 S.E. 240th St., Kent, 425-413-9614)

WEST VIRGINIA
Medical Centers:
*Beckley 25801 (200 Veterans Ave., 304-255-2121)
Clarksburg 26301 (1 Medical Center Dr., 304-623-3461 or 1-800-733-0512)
Huntington 25704 (1540 Spring Valley Dr., 304-429-6741)
#*Martinsburg 25401 (Route 9, 304-263-0811 or 1-800-817-3807)
Clinics:
Charleston 25304 (104 Alex Lane, 304-926-6001)
Franklin 26807 (Pendleton Community Care, 314 Pine St., PO Box 100, 304-358-2355)
Gassaway 26624 (617 River St., 304-364-5654)
Parkersburg 26101 (912 Market St., 304-422-5114)
Parsons 26287 (206 Spruce St., 304-478-2219)
Petersburg 26847 (Grant Mem. Hospital, Rt. 55 W., 304-257-1026, ext. 120)
Regional Office:
Huntington 25701 (640 Fourth Ave., statewide, 1-800-827-1000; counties of Brooke, Hancock, Marshall, Ohio, served by Pittsburgh, Pa., RO)
Vet Centers:
Beckley 25801 (101 Ellison Ave., 304-252-8220)
Charleston 25302 (521 Central Ave., 304-343-3825)
Huntington 25701 (3135 16th St. Rd., Suite 11, 304-523-8387)
#Martinsburg 25401 (900 Winchester Ave., 304-263-6776)

Morgantown 26508 (1083 Greenbag Rd., 304-291-4303)
Princeton 24740 (905 Mercer St., 304-425-5653)
Wheeling 26003 (1206 Chapline St., 304-232-0587)
National Cemeteries:
Grafton NC 26354 (431 Walnut St., 304-265-2044)
West Virginia NC 26354 (Rt. 2, Box 127, Grafton, 304-265-2044)

WISCONSIN
Medical Centers:
Madison 53705 (2500 Overlook Terrace, 608-256-1901)
#*Milwaukee 53295 (5000 W. National Ave., 414-384-2000)
*Tomah 54660 (500 E. Veterans St., 608-372-3971)
Clinics:
Appleton 54914 (10 Tri-Park Way, 920-831-0070)
Baraboo 53913 (626 14th St., 608-280-7038)
Beaver Dam 53916 (208 LaCrosse St., 608-280-7038)
Chippewa Falls 54729 (2503 County Hwy. I, 715-720-3780)
Cleveland 53015 (1205 North Ave., 920-693-3750)
Green Bay 54303 (141 Siegler St., 920-497-3126)
Janesville 53545 (111 N. Main St. 608-280-7038)
Kenosha 53140 (800 55th St., 262-653-9286)
LaCrosse 54601-3200 (2600 State Rd., 608-784-3886)
Loyal 54446 (PO Box 26, 141 North Main St., 715-255-9799)
Rhinelander 54501 (3716 Country Dr., #6, 715-362-4080)
Superior 54880 (3520 Tower Ave., 715-392-9711)
Union Grove 53182 (21425 Spring St., 262-878-7000)
Wausau 54401 (515 S. 32nd Ave., 715-842-2834)
Wisconsin Rapids 54494 (710 E. Grand Ave., 715-424-3844)
Regional Office:
Milwaukee 53214 (5400 W. National Ave.; statewide, 1-800-827-1000)
Vet Centers:
Madison 53703 (147 S. Butler St., 608-264-5342)
Milwaukee 53218 (5401 N. 76th St., 414-536-1301)
National Cemetery:
Wood NC 53295-4000 (5000 W. National Ave., Bldg. 1301, Milwaukee, 414-382-5300)

WYOMING
Medical Centers
*Cheyenne 82001 (2360 E. Pershing Blvd., 307-778-7550 or 1-888-483-9127)
*Sheridan 82801 (1898 Fort Rd., 307-672-3473)
Clinics:
Casper 82601 (111 South Jefferson St., Suite 105, 307-235-4143)
Gillette 82718 (1701 Phillips Circle, Suite A, 307-685-0676)
Green River 82935 (1400 Uinta Dr., 307-872-4508)
Newcastle 82701 (307-746-9533 or 1-800-764-5370)
Powell 82435 (777 Ave. H, 307-754-7257)

Riverton 82501 (2300 Rose Lane, 307-857-1211)
Benefits Office:
Cheyenne 82001 (2360 E. Pershing Blvd.; statewide, 1-800-827-1000)
Vet Centers:
Casper 82601 (111 S. Jefferson, Suite 100, 307-261-5355)
Cheyenne 82001 (2424 Pioneer Ave., Suite 103, 307-778-7370)

Index

Agent Orange 10, 20
Aid & Attendance 7, 12, 23, 53, 54,
Alcohol-Dependence Treatment 13
Allied Veterans 18
Appeals 59
 - Board of Veterans' Appeals 59
 - U.S. Court of Appeals for
   Veterans Claims 60
Armed Forces Retirement
 Home 71
Automobile Assistance 22
Beneficiary Travel 17
Benefit Payments 19
Benefit Programs 19
Birth Defects 26, 27, 76
Blind Veterans 12
Burial Benefits 4, 47
 - Headstones and Markers 48
 - Flags 49
Businesses
   - Small and Disadvantaged 58
   - Small Business Admin. 67
CHAMPVA 16, 17, 79
Clothing Allowance 22
Commissary Privileges 72
Compensated Work Therapy 13, 57
Copayments 7-10, 15
Correction of Military Records 71
Death Gratuity 72
Death Pension 53, 54, 76
Dependency and Indemnity Compensation (DIC) 52
 - Special Allowances 53
 - Restored Entitlement 53
 - Dependent & Survivor
   Medical Care 16, 17
Dependents Allowances 23
Dependents Education 27, 54, 55

Disability Compensation 4, 7, 19, 21, 23, 26, 57, 59
Discharge Reviews 69, 70
Domiciliary Care 16, 18, 24, 57
Drug-Dependence Treatment 13
Education and Training 28
Eligibility, General 1
Emergency Medical Care 17
Exchange Privileges 72
Federal Jobs for Veterans 64
Filipino Veterans 4, 47
Financial Assessment 8
Gulf War Veterans 2, 7, 10, 11, 14, 20, 38
Headstones and Markers 48
Health Care Benefits 6
Health Care Enrollment 6, 7
Home Improvements 12, 13
Housebound 7, 12, 23, 53, 54
Homeless Veterans 11, 14, 57, 62, 65
Improved Pension 24, 54
Incarcerated Veterans 23
Insurance
 - Accelerated Death Benefits 44
 - Billing Insurance Companies 10
 - Insurance Dividends 45
 - Life Insurance 43
 - Service-Disabled Veterans 44
 - Servicemembers' Group Life 43
 - Veterans' Group Life 44
 - Veterans' Mortgage Life 45
Ionizing Radiation 11, 14, 20
Iraqi Freedom Veterans 10, 11
Job-Finding Assistance 61-65
Loans
 - Farms and Homes 65
Home Loan
 - Eligibility 36
 - Closing Costs 40

- Financing, Rates, Terms 40
- Guaranties 36, 54
- Guaranty Amount 39
- Loan Assumption 41
- Native American Veterans 41
- Release of Liability 41
- Restored Entitlement 41
- Required Occupancy 39
- Safeguards 42

Medal of Honor Pension 24
Medals 69
Merchant Marine Seamen 3, 18
Military Funeral Honors 50-51
Montgomery GI Bill 28
- Death Benefit 56
- Selected Reserve 33

Naturalization Preference 66
Nursing-Home Care 15, 24
Outpatient Dental Treatment 13
Outpatient Pharmacy Services 14
Overseas Benefits 18, 58
Pension 23
Phone, Toll-free Numbers 78
Presidential Memorial
  Certificates 47, 49
Prisoners of War 7, 11, 13, 19, 38, 52, 54
Project SHAD 7, 14
Prosthetics and Sensory Aids 12
Radiation Exposure 7, 11, 14, 20
Re-employment Rights 63
Readjustment Counseling 11
Replacing Military Records 70
Repossessed Homes 42
Restored Survivors' Entitlement 53
Special Access to Care 8
Social Security 8, 24, 53, 54, 57, 67
Spanish Translation 5, 79
Special Groups 2-4
Specially Adapted Homes 12, 21-22

Spina Bifida Allowance 26, 76
Supplemental Security Income 68
Survivor Benefits 52
Tables 73
Transition Assistance Program 61
TRICARE 16
Unemployable Veterans 26
Unemployment Compensation 61
VA Facility Addresses & Phones 80
Veterans' Educational Assistance
  Program (VEAP) 34
Vocational and Educational Counseling 32-35, 55
- Rehabilitation & Employment 24
- Training for Children with Spina
  Bifida/Certain Birth Defects 27
Wartime Service 2
Women Veterans 1, 56
Workforce Investment Program 62
World Wide Web Links 79

U.S. GOVERNMENT PRINTING OFFICE
KEEPING AMERICA INFORMED

Federal Benefits for Veterans and Dependents 2005
Publication ORDER FORM

Easy Secure Internet:
bookstore.gpo.gov

Mail:
Superintendent of Documents
PO Box 371954
Pittsburgh, PA 15250-7954

Order Processing Code
3451

Toll Free: 866 512-1800
Phone: 202 512-1800
Fax: 202 512-2250

Charge your order, It's easy!

❑ **YES!** please send me_____copies of *Federal Benefits for Veterans and Dependents 2005*. S/N 051-000-00228-8, ISBN: 0-16-072420-1, single copies $7.00; $67.00/pack of 25.

The total cost of my order is $_____. Price includes regular postage and handling and price is subject to change. International customer please add 40%. Price subject to change without notice.

_____
Personal name   (Please type or print)

_____
Company name

_____
Street address

_____
City, State, Zip code

_____
Daytime phone including area code

❑ Check payable to *Superintendent of Documents*
❑ SOD Deposit Account ☐☐☐☐☐☐☐–☐
❑ VISA ❑ MasterCard ❑ Discover/NOVUS ❑ American Express

☐☐☐☐ ☐☐☐☐ ☐☐☐☐ ☐☐☐☐
☐☐☐☐ (expiration date)   *Thank you for your order!*

_____
Authorizing signature   02/05

ISBN 0-16-072420-1